Saul's Spear

Also By The Author

Ruth Uncensored

Saul's Spear

Breaking the Curse of Insecurity
that is
Ruining your Life and
Threatening your Legacy

Virginia Beach, Virginia

One Focus
1244 Thompkins Lane
Virginia Beach, VA 23464

Cover design: Orbit Graphics
Interior design: Nicole Cober-Lake

ISBN: 978-0-9997542-0-7 (Paperback)
ISBN: 978-0-9997542-1-4 (ebook)

Printed in the United States of America

First edition

To the congregation of Grace Covenant Church of Roanoke, who invested so much in me during the fourteen years I had the privilege of serving them.

Table of Contents

SECTION IV: The Insecure Parent

SECTION V: The Insecure Leader

Introduction

Over the years, I've started and stopped this book dozens of times. I've even tried to quit the project altogether. But recently, while standing in my driveway in a fit of frustration, I prayed, "Lord, do you want this book written? Is there really a need for it?" It was then that I felt the Lord communicate this to me:

He said, "Jeff, if My people could behave just this much less insecurely" – in my mind's eye I could see the Lord holding out his hand, with his thumb and forefinger about an inch or so apart – "we would all be a lot further along."

So there you have it. This is the great ambition of this book: that its readers would behave just a bit less insecurely.

The inspiration for the title and theme of this book comes from the multiple references to Saul's spear in the Biblical account of his life. Time and time again we're reminded that King Saul had a spear.

He clutched it when demonic powers assaulted his soul. He threw it at his son and successor, and held onto it while bullying his inner circle. He even slept with it. He leaned on it after his failed suicide attempt. And in the end, it was probably the weapon that was used to put him to death.

It's as if the Biblical author left us a literary clue, a signpost warning us of the dangers of following in Saul's footsteps. His spear photobombed into his biography, where his sad stories are piled like heavy stones one atop the other, an ancient cairn meant to turn us away from his disastrous route.

His spear was his scepter, the ever-present enforcer of his personal authority and constant reminder to those around him that he would defend his throne unto death. It was his security talisman that he brandished to intimidate others and fondled to comfort his own tormented soul.

His spear is an iconic reminder to every generation of the vanity and futility of maintaining and defending one's position, status, or authority apart from God. It is a reminder of the consequences of acting upon the feelings of self-doubt and inadequacy that beset us all – the crippling personality trait we moderns call insecurity.

Don't look for the word *insecurity* in the Bible. It's not there.

It wasn't until the beginning of the twentieth century that the word became a kind of catchall to explain and describe a host of negative behaviors and attitudes. Nonetheless, Saul's life reads like a textbook case of someone who suffers from a profound level of insecurity.

His career as Israel's first king starts out brilliantly, but just a few years after his coronation things begin to go very wrong. The self-effacing farmer anointed by the Spirit of God quickly turns into a bitter tyrant. Throughout his reign we find him armed and ready to do battle with anyone who would threaten his position or stand in his way. His insecurities twist and contort him into a man of extreme contradictions. Here are a few examples:

- He was better looking than his contemporaries, but thought himself inadequate.
- He was chosen by God to be king of Israel, but hides himself on the day of his coronation.
- He was imbued by the Spirit of God to deliver his nation from foreign oppression, but used that power to carry out his personal agendas.
- He was the tallest man in Israel, but when a warrior giant confronted his armies, he lent out his armor to a young shepherd with a nice complexion and a flair for music.
- He had a devoted son, but believed him to be a disloyal conspirator.
- He surrounded himself with Godly and talented leaders, but eyed them with suspicion and stymied their development.
- He was praised by his nation, but unable to laud the achievements of his subordinates.

There is no doubt that the life of King Saul is more cautionary tale than inspirational biography. Reading his story is painful. The pages of Scripture still feel wet with the tears of the prophet Samuel, who grieved over the man he anointed. The account sodden with the very regret of God, who made him king. It is the very sad story of a man who started well and finished poorly.

But perhaps the greatest tragedy of all is that once he becomes king and has the power to act upon those feelings, he does so with almost complete abandon. He represses, abuses, and even kills those who challenge him. Eventually he destroys even his own family, leaving a disastrous legacy in his wake.

Learning from his life is challenging. We'll never fully understand the world in which he lived. The sights and smells of his age are long forgotten and buried in the Middle Eastern earth. We know even less about Saul before he became king. Yet, even with the little we know about his family and the years before his reign, we see that his personhood was scarred by a deep sense of self-doubt and an inaccurate understanding of himself.

In spite of the three thousand years that separate us, Saul's story has the power to unearth the sources of insecurity in us. Along the way, we'll see things in Saul that bear a striking resemblance to ourselves and our own stories, so we'll have plenty of opportunity to discover and address the feelings and circumstances that give birth to our own insecurities. But be forewarned: unearthing the sources of our insecurities is not a prerequisite for turning away from the destructive behaviors they cause.

So before we launch into a closer examination of Saul's insecurities and the ways our own insecurities are negatively affecting us and those around us, it would be good for us to underscore the truth that we don't have to understand all the sources and causes of our insecurities to stop acting upon them.

In the same way that it's impossible to try to diagnose all of Saul's issues while standing three thousand years away, I believe it's just as impossible to think that we can ever completely know all the ingredients and circumstances that contribute to our own sense of insecurity. Yes, I believe by God's grace we will along the way discover more than enough insight about ourselves to allow us to love and lead those around us in a more secure and godly way. But more importantly, we will have the opportunity to first stop behaving insecurely when we recognize these behaviors in ourselves.

This is why the Scriptures are an essential ingredient in this process, and why each chapter of this book begins with a Scripture passage and a conversation about the life of Saul. The confluence of the ancient story, our present-day experience, and the Spirit of God is the place where our healing can begin.

This will undoubtedly be a difficult, and at times painful examination of our own feelings and behaviors. But thankfully, the Scriptures are the safe and sacred place where our names and our faces can be pasted into the stories of our spiritual ancestors. The sacred space where our unholiness, misunderstandings, distortions, illegitimate feelings, unrighteous desires, and ungodly ambitions can be disrobed and disarmed. The safe place to reflect upon the sources of our own insecurities and, in the process, become safer people.

I believe that if we have any legitimate hope of preparing, blessing, and releasing the next generation of leaders; of empowering our families; or of fulfilling our own destinies, we must be willing to exchange our insecurities for the security of knowing our value and worth apart from positions, titles, and even our own gifting. I believe we will then be able to turn fully away from the same kind of behaviors that sabotaged the life and legacy of King Saul.

What we're searching for is the grace and strength to lay down our own spears.

SECTION I:
The Insecure Soul

CHAPTER 1

The Problem of Insecurity

"By chance I happened to be on Mount Gilboa, and behold, Saul was leaning on his spear. And behold, the chariots and the horsemen pursued him closely...So I stood beside him and killed him, because I knew that he could not live after he had fallen."
— 2 Samuel 1:6-7, 10

Being assigned first-period gym class was embarrassing.

It meant having to hustle to the locker room and change into gym clothes the moment the bell rang at the start of the school day. While other kids were chatting with their friends and finding their way to class, I was fiddling with combination locks and changing into a smelly gym uniform. A uniform that included my older brother's ragged hand-me-down t-shirt that my mom had declared to be good enough. A size or two too-small shorts that I had been outgrowing since the eighth grade. A pair of socks that were once white, and black high-top canvas Converse All Stars – and trust me when I tell you that this was long before Chuck Taylors were cool.

Like most high school gym uniforms, ours were dull reminders of the bright colors worn by our school's state championship football team. The freshly laundered uniforms our varsity boys wore when they burst through the paper barrier at the entrance to the stadium on Saturday afternoons and ran the gauntlet of big-eyed cheerleaders who adoringly shook their pompoms for them. The team who wowed the fans who packed the stands that shook and rattled under the weight of all those stomping feet and clapping hands.

But of course there weren't any football players in first-period gym. Athletes were assigned to the prestigious seventh period gym class, the last class of the day, when jocks could take whirlpools and have their ankles taped before practice. The class when coaches allowed them to terrorize the handful of freaks and band guys who were the victims of scheduling glitches, and found themselves in a class where they were used as dodgeball fodder and twisted into wrestling match pretzels.

So even though first-period gym was safe, it was embarrassing to be in it. When schedules came out and your friends saw you had that class, they let out a sympathetic sigh. First-period gym was at the very bottom of the social-athletic caste, shattering any illusion a guy might have been harboring about an uptick in his physical prowess. Everyone also knew that first period gym would be forced outdoors when the autumnal sun was barely breaking over the horizon and parking lot puddles were still glassed over with plates of marbled ice.

We played flag football most of the fall. Then a couple of weeks before Thanksgiving, we switched over to soccer, the only sport that required enough running to keep us from freezing to death on those cold mornings. After attendance and leg lifts on the gymnasium floor, we donned blue and red pinnies and stumbled and shoved our way out into the wind and gray. We jogged past the football stadium, past the baseball diamonds; we jogged until we came to a stony and nearly grassless patch of earth at the farthest corner of the school's property.

Perhaps the only good thing about being in first-period gym class was that it allowed average athletes like myself the opportunity to shine just a little more brightly than we would have in other classes. For half an hour every morning, I could be the one-eyed king in the land of the blind, a slightly larger fish in a puddle of bespectacled National Honor Society guys. I suppose this was why I was playing center forward for the blue team on the Tuesday before Thanksgiving of my sophomore year.

On that morning, the sun was masked in thick overcast, and the air smelled of snow. We were suffering in the cold, our morale buoyed only by the thought that it was the eve of Thanksgiving break, and we took solace in the knowledge that a long weekend of eating and idling about lay ahead. The red and the blue slouched at opposing ends of the dirt like ragamuffin pawns on a frozen chess board. The whistle blew, and the match began. Coach was on the sidelines bundled in his varsity parka and sipping coffee from a Styrofoam cup while our naked thighs turned ever deeper shades of maroon.

About halfway through the match I was near midfield, attempting to receive a pass from a teammate when the ball got under my feet and I started to fall. Somehow, my skinny legs and the ball got tangled up in such an awkward way that before I hit the ground, my right femur broke. I instantly knew it was broken because of the loud, sickening sound it made when it snapped. It sounded like a thick branch being broken up for firewood in the crotch of a tree. Later, X-rays showed a completely severed bone just two inches below my hip socket.

After I fell, Coach blew his whistle and came and stood over me, and like most muscled gym teachers, he began barking orders.

"Get up and walk it off, Ell." I just lay there at his feet.

"It's broken," I said in a voice barely above a whisper.

"How do you know it's broken?" he asked.

I'm sure he was thinking that I was just another wuss who had skinned his knee and was trying to whine and cry his way into a nurse's note that would keep me from gym class for the next couple of weeks.

"I heard it" was the last thing I could get out of my mouth.

He leaned over for a closer look, carefully holding his coffee to the side. Then a truly frightened look came across his face. He stood up and yelled at some of the bigger guys to go get the stretcher and the nurse. When they slid me from the earth to the stretcher, I was too weak to cry out, and for the life of me couldn't understand why I was lathered in sweat on such a cold morning.

The rescue squad and my mom got to the school at the same time, and they let her ride in the back of the ambulance on the way to the hospital. Later that day, I was taken into surgery, where orthopedic surgeons drilled a big hole into the socket ball of my hip and inserted a steel plate that was fastened to the lower part of my thigh with six screws that went nearly all the way through the bone. Finally, they wrapped my leg, hips, and lower torso in a chest-high cast. I awoke in the recovery room six hours later, trapped in a plaster sarcophagus.

I spent the next week craving the injections of morphine that deadened the unbearable ache radiating from the core of my body. Every three hours I awoke from my stupor as an alarm went off in my brain and I began to count off the minutes until I got my next fix. The nurses would come to my bedside, hold up the syringe, and squeeze a few drops out while I watched in anticipation. They would gently roll me to my side to stick me in my un-plastered left buttock, and push the plunger. The pain would instantly start to fade. Most of the nurses were motherly, and after the injection would say things like, "There you go, sweetie...now you can go back to sleep."

After a couple of weeks in the hospital, Mom and Pop had a hospital bed delivered to the house and set it up in the dining room. Another ambulance took me back to our house, and I was wheeled into the dining room on a gurney. They slid me onto the waiting hospital bed, where I spent the next four months lying on my back while my bone knit back together. The school employed tutors who came to the house to teach my classes. *Bedpans* and *boredom* are the two words that come to mind when I think about that winter.

The following year, I had a second surgery to remove the plate and the screws. Thanks to my mom, who was a great nurse, and the doctors who operated on me, I healed very well. Other than these memories, only three things remain: a nearly foot-long scar that runs the length of my thigh, a dull ache when the weather turns bad, and an occasional limp.

It's a very slight limp; most folks wouldn't ever notice it, but I know it's there because the soles of my shoes wear out unevenly. And after a long hike, or if I carry a heavy load for a while, it becomes more pronounced. Even though I healed well, my once-broken right leg is still smaller and weaker than my left leg.

I'm pretty sure that right about now, you're wondering why I'm telling you a story about a clumsy kid who broke his leg during a meaningless gym class soccer match on a cold November morning in a book about the insecurities and the death of Israel's first king. There are a few good reasons, which we will look at in more detail soon, but the first and perhaps the most important reason is:

To get us to slow down.

It's possible that you were hoping this book would offer some sort of self-help 'how-to' formula. A recipe that would enable you to quickly and painlessly overcome the insecurities that afflict your soul. A pit stop of sorts that would swap out the worn-out tires, wipe your windshield, and send you back out on the lead lap of life with clear vision and a full tank of confidence and security.

Or maybe you're thinking this book could serve as a mail-order prescription that could be left anonymously on your boss's desk, or on your pastor's front step, and that if they would just read two pages before bedtime each night, they would wake up cured from their insecurities that are making your life so very difficult.

Sorry, this is not a self-help book. This is a God-help-me book.

So before we go any further, and before we start our look at Saul's life, it would be good to take a deep breath, let it out slowly, and accept the fact that no book, no sermon, no seminar, and no counseling session will instantaneously fix our insecurities. Like a badly broken leg, some things take time to heal, and may even need some intentional and intense intervention along the way.

It would also be right for us to tip our caps to acknowledge that all of us are exposed to more than enough reasons, both legitimate and illegitimate, to feel insecure. The age in which we live is being carpet-bombed by messages, images, injustices, and societal forces that shatter identities and collapse the relationships and family structures that are meant to be our greatest sources of security. If someone were to invent an insecurity detector, a device that could be waved over people like a Geiger counter, everyone would get a number. All of us seem to have some kind of insecurity kicking around in our souls. Of course, some folks would definitely get a higher number than others. For a few, insecurity is the single most life-controlling issue they are dealing with. It's become so pronounced that they're at a place where they know they need to address it now, because it's isolating them from God, injuring the ones they love, and sabotaging their success.

And while insecure people definitely seem to be more sensitive than others, it's not their intention or choice to be this way. Like high-speed film or wet sand, images and impressions are made upon them more quickly and easily; criticism is more readily taken to heart, and the fear of rejection felt more intensely than for the average person. So let's not race to the premature conclusion that feeling insecure means that we must have done something wrong. But it's why the best looking guy on campus can look into his mirror and wonder if he is man enough, and why the prettiest girl in the neighborhood can look into her mirror and see nothing but imperfections and unattractiveness. It's why the most talented actors, the most gifted musicians, and the most powerful politicians find themselves doubting their abilities after a bad review or an unflattering remark from a commentator. Even the most devout and earnest believers can find themselves questioning the reality and authenticity of their relationship with God.

If this describes you and your current struggle, I'm glad you're reading this, and I'm confident that you will soon start to become free from these life-controlling behaviors and feelings. I'm optimistic that by looking at the life of Saul through the lens of insecurity, all of us will be able to recognize insecurities in our own lives more readily and recoil from them more quickly, as we allow the Spirit of God to illuminate the Scriptures and change our view of ourselves and the people around us.

If you don't know much about Saul yet, it's ok. For now it's enough to know that he was the first king of ancient Israel, and that he was the tallest and best looking guy in the land. He was called by God and anointed by the prophet Samuel to lead the nation. Almost immediately after his calling, the Spirit of God came upon him, and he experienced a transformation so supernatural that the Bible says he was turned into a different man. He worshiped and fellowshipped with a prophetic community that was eccentric and musical. In the first months of his reign, he burned with righteous indignation and rescued a besieged city by courageously leading the army into battle. After the victory, he graciously forgave his critics and detractors and led his nation in worship.

Sadly, this is the same man who then went on to destroy his family, turned away from God, was beset by demonic spirits, and led the nation astray. The same man who carried his spear wherever he went, and likely died with it thrust through his body. And while we'll never know all the whys of Saul's demise, we do have a long list of the hows.

But before we look more closely at Saul's story, it would be good for us to have a firmer grasp on our modern understanding of this thing we call insecurity and the potential dangers of allowing those feelings and impressions to dominate our lives.

Defining Insecurity

The word *insecurity* was first used in our modern sense in 1917. In less than one hundred years, this word, pregnant with emotional and psychological meaning, has found its way into the common language of everyday life. Honestly, I'm not sure how the human race got along without it for so long, but its rise from obscurity is due to the fact that it is the one word that best captures all those feelings and behaviors that have been afflicting humanity ever since the first couple ran for the bushes.

Insecurity is one of those things that's not easy to fully define, yet everyone seems to be able to recognize it when they see it. The vagaries of the term have made it a psychological catchall, a none-too-subtle dig that can be penciled in as the underlying root of nearly every behavioral or emotional foible that we, or someone else, fall prey to. But just so we are on the same page and have a common working definition to start from, let's look to a modern authority for a solid definition of insecurity. Dr. Joseph Nowinski defines it this way:

> Insecurity refers to a profound sense of self-doubt, a deep feeling of uncertainty about our basic worth and

> our place in the world. Insecurity is associated with chronic self-consciousness, along with chronic lack of confidence in ourselves and anxiety about our relationships. The insecure man or woman lives in constant fear of rejection and a deep uncertainty about whether his or her own feelings and desires are legitimate.[1]

I really appreciate this carefully crafted definition because it captures two sobering facts about insecurity that we will see on full display in the life of Saul. First, insecurity rarely, if ever, stays confined to our secret inner lives. Left unaddressed, these feelings and anxieties invariably escape and damage our relationships with others. Second, Dr. Nowinski uses the word *chronic* twice. This points to the reality that insecurity involves constant fear, an ongoing and often life-long struggle with the dread of rejection and with a sense of legitimacy. Like Saul, the profoundly insecure find themselves like fugitives on the lam, forever looking over their shoulders and living in constant fear that one day there will be a knock at the door.

According to one tradition, the Chinese language might have the best way of writing *insecurity*. It may involve two symbols: the first means "phobia in high place," and the second means "origin or beginning." It's like a screenshot of the insecure soul, a word picture that tells the story of the fears that percolate from the core of our beings and fill us with self-doubt and inadequacy. Two pictures that are perhaps an intuitive glimpse of what Adam and Eve were feeling as they fumbled about in the undergrowth with the first needle and thread.

Symbols and pictures seem to do a better job than words of capturing the essence of the thing we call insecurity. This is why Saul's story and the images from his life are so effective at illustrating and communicating what insecurity actually looks like.

Also, for the purpose of future conversations, I would like to use the phrase *profound insecurity* to describe a level of insecurity that actually manifests in destructive behaviors. Behaviors so pronounced that they threaten the well-being of both individuals and the people around them. We have already mentioned that insecurity is a nearly universal human experience, that virtually everyone can recognize it and has at some point in their lives probably felt some of its effects.

---

[1] Nowinski, Joseph. *The Tender Heart: Conquering Your Insecurity*. Simon and Schuster, 2001, p. 23.

But don't look for the word *insecurity* in the Bible – it's not there, and there's no chapter and verse we can quote that tells us Saul was insecure. Yet even the casual observer will see that he is the veritable poster child for our modern understanding of the word. The narrative of his life is like old home movies where we get to catch a few jittery glimpses of our spiritual ancestor as he continued his tragic decline.

But regardless of the definition we settle on, we'll soon see that the consequences for anyone – and especially those with authority and influence in the lives of others – of acting upon these feelings are catastrophic at worst, and problematic at best.

Dangers of Insecurity

An old injury that causes a bit of a limp is a really good metaphor to describe how insecurities bother most of us. Somewhere along the way we get tangled up in something, or someone trips or pushes us; we fall, something breaks, and we are left with a scar or wound that nags us for the rest of our lives. Like the story of my busted leg, nearly everyone has a similar tale about something traumatic or painful that happened to them in the past yet still has some kind of lingering effect on them today. This is why feeling insecure is something virtually every human being can relate to.

It's unlikely that everyone experiences the same amount of insecurity, or at the very least, not everyone acts upon those insecurities in the same way. I'm not sure exactly when insecurity levels become dangerous. In a way that's similar to how our bodies cope with tiny levels of toxins, we seem to be able to cope with small bits of insecurity. For most of us, our insecurities are not on public display; they are more like the quiet hum of an appliance running harmlessly in the background of our lives. They usually don't activate or become amplified until we find ourselves in a new or unfamiliar role or situation. At some point, a threshold is breached, and all those feelings rush upon us and threaten both us and those around us.

Insecurities are so very dangerous because they have a nasty way of manifesting at the most critical junctures in our lives. Like a blackhead on the morning of our wedding or a nick from the razor on the day of a big interview, they seem to afflict us the most right when we need them the least. Insecurities have the ability to incubate in the human soul for long periods of time, only to awaken in us as we arrive at these crucial junctures, and when the people we lead and love need us the most.

This is how it was for Saul.

He is a perfect example of someone whose insecurities didn't fully manifest until he entered into his new position. Early on, we have several clues that insecurity was going to be a major issue in his life, but it's not until he becomes king that he acts upon them. The same thing is true for most of us; under normal circumstances, the manifestations and indications of insecurity are often so subtle that they escape notice. Then when fresh or unusual stress happens, a fissure is created, a crack through which the once-dormant insecurities escape and bubble to the surface.

My assumption is that some of you reading this are already convinced that this examination of King Saul's insecurities is not especially relevant to you. You're confident in both who you are and what you're called to do, and that is wonderful. But before you take it off the queue on your electronic reader or put it back on the shelf, be aware that insecurities really do have a curious way of lying dormant, and then suddenly and unexpectedly becoming animated when we find ourselves in a new position or on unfamiliar territory.

If I might be so bold, I would like to suggest that it's naive and maybe even arrogant to assume that our latent insecurities could never manifest into something more harmful than they are now. There are just too many examples of well-meaning men and women, just like Saul, whose insecurities suddenly erupted into something much more dangerous than a nagging limp.

For these folks, a darker metaphor seems in order. A deadly disease or cancer comparison seems more fitting. These are those Saul-like souls whose manifestations of insecurity are so acute that it handicaps them in their daily lives and is ruining their most important relationships. They have become trapped in a cycle of neediness and control that is so intense that they quickly drain the limited resources of their families and friends, who discover that they cannot meet the constant desire for affirmation and attention that the profoundly insecure demand.

An old Irish preacher once told me that insecurity was "a dog that can't be fed," meaning that no matter how much attention and affirmation you give insecure people, it's never enough, and soon they will be whimpering or growling for more. The profoundly insecure are driven by an insatiable appetite; they experience a nearly constant ache in the belly of their soul and seek to have their hunger sated in all sorts of unhealthy and destructive ways.

To keep their own emotional and spiritual sanity, the people closest to the profoundly insecure are eventually forced to retreat to a safe distance. They stop returning phone calls, they avoid them after church, sometimes they even work longer hours at their jobs to avoid going home to them. Then the cycle starts again. The insecure misinterprets their family and friends' inability to provide what they want as evidence of even more rejection. Some have compared this emotional loop to being trapped on a bus at an airport. A bus that stops at the same terminals, turns the same direction, and completes the same circuit every hour of every day of every year.

In an attempt to stop the cycle, the profoundly insecure will often try to control the people around them. They adopt a Big Brother mentality to govern their relationships. This kind of governance requires constant vigilance, so they become the private security firm of their family, church, and business. And while they probably don't monitor a wall of television screens from hidden cameras (though they might), they do monitor the conversations, movements, friendships, and behaviors of those around them. They use others as informants to gather information, all the while looking for any hint of disloyalty or faltering allegiances in their spheres.

The controlling grip of the profoundly insecure will eventually push people out of their lives, causing their world to shrink with each squeeze. Eventually, they may become withdrawn, isolated, lethargic, and unable to muster the courage to attempt new things or new relationships that have any chance of failure. They shuffle through life hobbled by all manner of fears, continually second guessing decisions and doubting their own abilities and judgments.

Perhaps a warning label should be pasted on Saul's story – something like the information on the back of drain openers and household chemicals with bold slashes through big red circles, and grisly illustrations of hands being chemically dissolved. But on the off chance we still need a few more reasons to pay attention to the potential hazards of acting on our insecurities, here is a partial list of the dangerous and controlling things insecure people do:

- They sabotage the lives of those they perceive to be a threat to their position or status
- They protect their reputations at the expense of relationships
- They hinder and delay the development of subordinates
- They enact destructive rules and regulations
- They continue in their offices and positions after they are no longer effective
- They sacrifice family to accomplish their goals

- They ignore sound advice and are dismissive of the ideas of others
- They misuse resources for personal vendettas
- They engage in self aggrandizement
- They jeopardize their legacy

But fear not! The good news is that secure people do just the opposite! The Holy Spirit is all about setting us free from all of our insecurities. So before we get too discouraged, here is a quick list of things secure people do:

- They help launch those around them into greater spheres of success
- They are transparent and allow those around them to know them intimately
- They follow the prophetic words God has given them
- They train and develop future leaders
- They allow their institutions to be governed by the Spirit of God
- They move out of ineffective roles and positions in a timely manner
- They correctly value the importance of their families
- They receive counsel and are open to new ideas
- They have little concern for the material trappings of success
- They ensure a long-lasting legacy
- They glorify God

Increasing Insecurities

Not only are insecurities dangerous, but they seem more prevalent than ever. One of the factors that has lent its energy to this uptick of insecurity is that an increasing number of people are living alone, or living without meaningful community, than ever before. The normal social fabric meant to undergird us has been growing weaker and weaker, and ever increasing numbers of people no longer have the nurturing support of family and close community.

In his book *Going Solo: The Extraordinary Rise and Surprising Appeal of Living Alone*, sociologist Eric Klinenberg has documented this growing segment of our culture, a demographic he refers to as "singletons," calling their lifestyle the "biggest unnamed social change of the last 50 or 60 years that we have failed to name or identify."[2]

Not only are more people living alone, but an ever larger percentage of us are also living with companions and family members from whom we receive little or no emotional or spiritual support. Married couples who live under the same roof only because their economic situation does not allow them the luxury of separation, and children who find themselves disconnected from meaningful interaction with their parents – these are just a couple of ready examples of the growing demographic of those who find themselves increasingly isolated from the kinds of relationships that enable us to better navigate the dangerous currents and tides of modern life.

It's a perfect storm of sorts: the coming together of powerful societal fronts has created a cultural climate that is ideal for spawning the behaviors and feelings we call insecurity. Our cultural landscape has become an ideal location for those insecurities to develop into powerful and destructive behavioral tornadoes that rip the roofs off churches and send families running for the basement.

Psychological Route

When I first embarked on this exploration of Saul's life through the lens of insecurity, I started reading books, blogs, and magazine articles, and discovered most of them were written from a distinctly psychological perspective. The more I read, the more I felt like I was back in my senior year in college, taking the social science research class that recommended a course in statistics as a prerequisite. The statistics class wasn't required, just recommended, but the professor had cautioned us that it would be difficult to pass without it. I never took statistics, and somehow managed to pass that class, but I was really, really confused most of that semester. Yet escaping from the clutches of insecurity isn't the same as passing a class. The stakes are so much higher.

So as I pushed deeper into all that material, I started feeling less like a clueless student and more like a trekker who had gone missing in a deep jungle and was trying to make his way downriver to the sea to be rescued. I could hear the sound of the surf crashing on the beach occasionally, but I kept getting turned around in the tangle of mangrove swamps where all the streams and coves look the same. All that information steeped in psychological terms became like a

---

[2] Klinenberg, Eric. "Why More Americans Are Living Alone." Interview by Ray Suarez. *PBS Newshour*. 27 Mar. 2012. Television.

vast and muddy river delta to me, an untraversable estuary of observation and self-help suggestions whose turbid currents promised escape, but in the end only carried me deeper into the brackish backwaters. What I really needed was a local guide.

This is where Saul can come to the rescue of all of us. His life as depicted in the Scriptures is like an ancient map that shows us the dead end branches of the river and sandbars that can keep us from reaching the sea. As we travel alongside the man who seems to be the very embodiment of insecurity, we can discover our own path to greater security. His life is a lens that can bring all those fuzzy feelings and ideas into focus, his story a biographical GPS that can chart our route.

Perhaps there are some folks who have escaped the jungle of insecurity by sorting out all the psychological information and opinions, then successfully plumbing the depths of their own psyches to make their way to safety. But I'm not one of them. So I applaud those rare individuals, whoever they are, who have the ability to process and act upon all that information. I have the same kind of admiration for people who can just pick up and solve the Rubik's Cube. But I think the vast majority of us find it nearly impossible to glean much practical guidance from these well-meaning, albeit confusing and often contradictory psychological opinions.

Insecurity is as old as Eden, and so it has a distinctly spiritual component. The self-doubt, fear, and all of its other facets are not confined to our minds, so these feelings overflow and spill over into all the other areas of our lives and relationships, including our relationship with God. This is why a psychological solution alone is unlikely to free us from the grips of insecurity.

A partial explanation for our heavy reliance and focus on the psychology of feelings and behaviors is that Psychology 101 or its equivalent has been a required course for undergraduate studies both here in America and in Europe for many years now. Some high schools and secondary schools have been offering similar classes for nearly as long. These curricula have given most of us a working vocabulary of behaviors and issues that are distinctly psychological, and so we readily talk about our feelings, emotions, and behaviors in a jargon that would have been unknown to our ancestors. Even as non-professionals, we readily observe and even try to diagnose a whole host of disorders in ourselves and others. Sit in any coffee shop and you'll overhear customers say things like "I'm neurotic," "She is an enabler," or "He has childhood wounding" without so much as a raised eyebrow or tilted head. We've become, without even noticing, a community highly fluent in the tongues of the counselor and the psychiatrist.

We regularly use psychological words in imprecise ways. Words that we think we know the meaning of, or feel we know the meaning of, but when we attempt to craft a singular definition with crisp edges, we soon discover that most of these words are just dull oral icons of the murky, yet universal feelings, fears, and impressions of the human experience. Insecurity is not unique in this sense; it is just one of perhaps dozens of words with psychological underpinnings and cloudy definitions that have found their way into our everyday conversations. Riding the wave of this vocabulary is the pseudo-psychology phenomenon, the unending parade of news stories, online personality tests, blogs, magazine articles, and interviews with experts which fill the demand for information and advice in a culture that seems obsessed with discovering and uncovering all the nuances of our mental, relational, and emotional experience.

Yet my snarky and cynical observation is this: If purely psychological explanations and solutions worked, surely by now, with so much information, with so much awareness, with so many trained counselors, we should have a reasonable expectation that insecurities and the like should be on the decline. But they are not. If anything, we seem to be inundated by emotional and mental issues, and purely psychological solutions look to be little more than berms of sand built on the beach by industrious children. Ditches and dykes dug by the plastic shovels of the sons of Adam are not capable of holding back the tide of fears and doubts that are flooding our culture.

Ultimately, we need a transformation, a realignment that takes place when our spirits and souls are exposed to the words of Scripture. And then, as we prayerfully consider the impressions and personal revelations we receive along the way, we will find ourselves engaged in the healing process. This is why a devotional and conversational look at the life of Saul through the lens of insecurity has the ability to help us escape the labyrinth of the psychological. Simply put, I believe the Word and the Spirit are our best hope of escaping the powerful curse of insecurity.

The Curse of Insecurity

You've probably noticed that we just used the word *curse* to describe insecurity. A curse is not just some mumbo-jumbo that a witch mutters over a cauldron of boiling brew or pin-stuck doll. It's much more harmful than any of that.

A curse is a persistent and ongoing bent to behave or think in an ungodly and harmful way. It's a behavior or limp in our souls that seems to flare up when we are under a particularly heavy burden or have been asked to walk in a new role. A curse is a weak place in the fabric of our beings that rips open and causes us to say and do things we ought not say and do.

A curse is a also a persistently unwholesome appetite to experience something we were not meant for. A curse is a behavioral or attitudinal pattern that is deeply rooted in our belief systems, and that is often wrapped around a destructive pattern in our personal family histories. A curse is a bad way of thinking that leads to bad behaviors.

Insecurity is a curse. It is a profound and deeply rooted sense of self-doubt that can motivate us to behave in such ungodly ways that we have the potential to sabotage our lives in a way similar to the way in which the curse of insecurity sabotaged the life of King Saul.

Feeling insecure is not a sin. It's just a feeling, sometimes justified, most of the time not.

Like any other feeling, the sin doesn't happen until we act upon it. Temptation is not a sin. When I feel lazy, I'm not participating in the sin of sloth until I balk at doing the things I'm supposed to do.

Insecurity is just a perception, usually a skewed understanding about who we are and what we are worth. And while insecurity is not a sin, make no mistake about it – insecurities can cause us to sin in some pretty horrific ways. As in Saul's life, our misperceptions about ourselves can spawn both willful disobedience and prideful actions that can cause us to reap catastrophic consequences. Our insecurities even have the potential to fuel a fire of rage and murderous grudge-bearing.

They say every journey starts with a step. So to begin our journey with Saul to become free from the destructive power of insecurity, we'll have to take the first step. And here is the first step:

Stop behaving insecurely.

I know it sounds crazy and counterintuitive, but give me just a second to explain how this works.

Curses are not broken just because we understand where they come from, any more than understanding the source of a disease cures it. Our generation has often labored under the wrongheaded belief that we must first understand the source of our sin or destructive behavior before we can stop doing inappropriate and sinful things. I believe just the opposite. I believe that when we stop acting on inappropriate feelings, we are taking the first step in understanding and identifying the issues and roots of many of these feelings.

When we stop doing ungodly and inappropriate things, even if it's just for an hour or a day, we experience life without the temporary intoxication and anesthetizing effect that a particular sin brings to us. For example, an insecure leader may think it expedient to burden a subordinate with a nearly impossible task, so as to injure their reputation and discredit them in their role. (Later we will see that Saul did this very thing.) But when they resist the urge to assign such a task or create an impossible goal, they are compelled to deal with their underlying fear of being replaced by younger talent. Facing that kind of fear without acting on it can be very painful.

In this sense, sin is also an analgesic. Like aspirin taking away a headache, sin temporarily takes away the fears, boredom, cravings, and anxieties that are often the precursors to willful disobedience or negligence. Without the analgesic of sin, we are faced with the unmasked pain of our true mental and spiritual state and have more ready access to the more deeply rooted core issues that have persistently plagued us.

Ultimately, the best chance we have of escaping the power of any destructive behavior will involve some understanding of the sources and dealing with the very roots of those issues. And the best way to get to those roots and fountainheads is by fully experiencing the raw pain they cause. The unmasked pain provides us with a window of opportunity, a first-step moment when we can choose not to engage in disobedience. The discomfort of holiness often gives us the best opportunity to correctly identify the specific fear, faulty belief system, or illegitimate expectation that has cursed us with seemingly uncontrollable desires.

Unfortunately, the wrongheaded assumption that understanding and identification must precede a change in behavior is in some measure responsible for the pandemic of insecure leaders, spouses, and parents who wield the weapons of their authority to maintain their status and position. The wholesale acceptance of the unbiblical belief that we must first understand the sources of our sins before we can stop sinning has given rise to an entire generation of often churlish souls who remain locked in dysfunction and rebellion.

Pausing the pursuit of God and right living in an attempt to discover the sources of our fears and proclivities is a fool's errand. Like pilgrims without maps and sailors without compasses, we wander spiritual deserts and roam vacant seas searching for emotional El Dorados and psychological Atlantises. Meanwhile, those who need our secure leadership the most pace their widow's walks as the chaos continues in homes, organizations, churches, and businesses. Potential leaders are injured, families dissected, and institutions scuttled by the neverending parade of interpersonal offense and moral failures that roil up from the fountainhead of insecurity.

But lest you think that I believe understanding and insight are not important, let me say clearly that they are, and that they are key elements in our development and maturation into secure people. The fact that repentance precedes insight does not in any way diminish the importance of discovering and understanding the incorrect beliefs that are prompting us to engage in destructive behaviors.

Put in simple Biblical language: repentance precedes salvation. If we embrace a Biblical understanding of salvation, which includes not just our eternal destiny but also the redemption of our souls in this present age, then we should find it unsurprising that our turning aside from manifestations of insecurity will be a precursor to our eventual discovery of the sources of those insecurities.

Once the ambulance got me to the hospital, it didn't take long for the emergency room doctors to figure out that my leg was broken. A correct diagnosis was essential in my treatment, and I'm really glad they didn't misdiagnose me with halitosis and send me home with a bottle of mouthwash. I'm just being silly here to underscore the fact that it wasn't the diagnosis that fixed my leg. It was a necessary first step for sure, and the X-rays that looked beneath my flesh guided the surgeons' scalpels. But in the end it was the steel plate, the plaster cast, and the God-given ability of the human body to knit bone back together that healed me. This is why just discovering and diagnosing the sources of our insecurities is not enough to heal us. We require divine intervention. We need God's help to become the secure people He created us to be.

Not an Indictment

My hope is that a few of the insights and thoughts we share will prompt an ongoing conversation of sorts, a safe and anonymous place where we can receive gentle course corrections when we lose our bearings. I want these words to become a safe place to walk, talk, and even laugh a little about the mysteries and complexities of life in a loving, dispassionate, and non-adversarial way. And oh my, if there ever were a set of feelings and behaviors that could be categorized as complicated, mysterious, and in need of some laughter to cheer us along the way, insecurities would certainly be at or near the top of that list.

Be forewarned – I'll continue to use some pretty strong language and graphic illustrations to depict Saul's struggle. The life of Saul shouldn't be sanitized and dressed up to make it more presentable to priggish religious culture. To be honest and fair with the text, we can't dip his story in the chocolate sprinkles of cheery pseudo-spiritual slogans. Saul's story is not for the faint of heart; if all but the first few years of his reign as king were distilled into a scratch-n-sniff, it would smell like crap.

I also want you to know that my only expertise on the subject of insecurity comes from some of my own deeply rooted tendencies to feel insecure. I didn't know if I should even attempt to write this book. I didn't know if it would help people. I'm sure it's not very good, and I'm convinced that my credentials to write about such a complicated topic are completely inadequate. I'm also afraid that someone will give it a bad review or say mean things about me... Like I said, we need to laugh a little along the way. But seriously, all teasing aside, I'm pretty sure my personal experiences will not remedy your insecurities either.

I'm just a guy who was reading his Bible one morning and realized how often Saul was pictured with his spear. Then, as I began to use my imagination to see myself doing and thinking some of the things Saul did and thought, I began to recognize some of the those same insecurities in myself that I hadn't noticed before. So I started to stop acting on my insecure feelings. That starting to stop we've already talked about, and the pain it caused, eventually helped me identify some of the origins of my own insecurities.

If you don't get anything else from this book, get this: Remember the Lord saying to me, "Jeff, if My people could behave just this much less insecurely" – when in my mind's eye I could see the Lord holding out his hand, with his thumb and forefinger about an inch or so apart – "we would all be a lot further along." Just an inch apart. I think that kind of distance takes the pressure off.

I don't believe a crash course in insecurity is going to help us be more secure, any more than a crash diet will help us permanently lose weight. I pray that you will soon arrive at a place where, when faced with the temptation to engage in some Saul-like behavior, you'll have the courage and security to stop acting on those feelings long before they injure, and possibly do irrevocable damage to yourself and those around you. My hope is that by sharing Saul's story here, we might start sharing our own stories with our families and friends.

You will soon see that each section begins with a passage of Scripture. Please take the time to read and enjoy the beautiful narrative and even read entire sections right from the Bible. This look at Saul's life is not even close to being a comprehensive or complete biography; there is so much more to his story than this short book could ever cover. My expectation is that as readers muse and meditate on the life of Saul, all kinds of Spirit-inspired thoughts and prayers are going to happen, and that thoughtful and prayerful readers are going to observe things along the trail with Saul that I never saw. I encourage you to enter his story, go ahead and paste your face on his and let the Spirit reveal things in you along the way.

You'll also notice that at the end of each section I've provided a few prayer and conversation-starting questions, meant to be a few thoughts for personal reflection and friendly sharing. Not only will you see things I've never seen, but you'll probably come up with better questions than I ask. My only request is that if you happen to use this as part of a group study or discussion, please keep it friendly. The worst thing that could happen is that someone would feel accused and condemned as they talk about this, because those feelings are going to make it way more difficult to become free from the power and influence of insecurity.

Be nice to your friends! Be kind to yourself! Grab your walking stick and a bottle of water, and let's jump into our Scriptural time machine and travel back to meet this man we've been talking about.

SECTION II:
The Insecure Believer

CHAPTER 2

Humble Beginnings

> *Now it came about on the next day that an evil spirit from God came mightily upon Saul, and he raved in the midst of the house, while David was playing the harp with his hand, as usual; and a spear was in Saul's hand. Saul hurled the spear for he thought, "I will pin David to the wall." But David escaped from his presence twice.*
> *— 1 Samuel 18:10-11*

When I read Saul's story, I get nervous. I feel like a child listening to his favorite bedtime book, still scared every time his dad shows him the pictures of fire-breathing dragons or children who have gotten lost in the woods. Even though I've read Saul's story hundreds of times, it still gives me the creeps when I see these scenes played out in my mind. Maybe it wouldn't be so scary if I knew his story had a happily-ever-after ending.

Most of us probably feel the same way when we read about Peter's denials of Jesus, Noah's binger, and David's philandering with Bathsheba. We want to yell at the Bible and shout across the chasm of time: "DON'T DO IT!" "TURN AROUND!" "QUOTE SCRIPTURE!" "PHONE YOUR ACCOUNTABILITY PARTNER RIGHT NOW!"

It's painful to turn the pages of the Bible in these places. It's hard to watch as these heroes of the faith inch ever closer to the edge of the precipice where they stumble, then tumble headlong into a canyon of consequences that are far worse than they ever imagined.

Saul's life is full of these scenes. All those times when he made bad choices and did stupid, and sometimes even evil things. For me, the most wrenching episodes of all are those that tell us about his spiritual journey. Passages of Scripture that tell about him raving in his house while an evil spirit is terrorizing him. And all the while he's got that damned spear in his hand.

This is why every time I read the story of Saul, I keep hoping it will change. That one day I will open up my Bible and discover that his nightmare has been replaced by a dreamy alternative. Like in one of those sci-fi movies when the space-time continuum gets altered and we think to ourselves, "Whew, for a moment there I thought the captain was dead and the science officer really was an evil warlord." I want to read about Saul living out his golden years surrounded by his grandchildren, tending his cucumber garden, and occasionally traveling to Jerusalem to be part of official ceremonies that needed the personal touch of the emeritus king. But this is not how his story ends.

As Saul grows old, we discover he's spiritually diseased. The years of disobedience and unbelief have spread through his entire being like an aggressive cancer. He doesn't worship. He's demonized. He consults witches. He's a total wreck. The initial short season of his healthy anointed days are just a distant memory, and the sickly and sinister years that he is best remembered for have settled in. Dark years, when he lost his ability to communicate with God and walk by faith.

In this section we'll look at the distinctly spiritual set of insecurities that plagued the life of Saul. We'll consider how our own spiritual insecurities impact us perhaps more deeply than all of our other insecurities combined. How many, if not all of our conversations and considerations of other facets of insecurity are going to prompt us to examine our own spiritual condition.

While insecurity is a nearly universal human experience, there are some insecurity issues that are unique in the life of the Christian. My hope is that some of you reading this book don't yet share my Christian perspective, and I'm really glad you've taken the time to explore the subject of insecurity through the porthole of Saul's life. So I want to give those readers an honest and respectful heads-up about how in this section we will look at some of the issues of faith that might seem distant or even irrelevant if you're not yet a believer.

I'm thoroughly convinced that most, if not all of the other places where our insecurities emerge are in essence manifestations or symptoms of insecurities rooted in our spiritual condition. Insecurities are like crabgrass in this respect; they sprout up in one place, but their roots are somewhere else. And more often than not, that somewhere else is our spiritual lives. The unseen place of faith, where our spirits mingle with the Spirit of God.

This understanding might go the furthest in explaining why insecurities seem to continually pop back up in spite of our best efforts to eradicate them. Like Saul, we make promises with tears running down our cheeks to stop hunting the metaphorical Davids in our own lives. Then not too long afterward, we find ourselves hot on his trail again, returning to the same feelings and behaviors that we've tried so often to abandon.

I'm not going to suggest or pretend that by examining the life of Saul we'll discover some simplistic explanation for why humans sin. Not all sin is directly related to insecurity. Everyone's story has its own unique twists and turns, and human beings are wonderfully complicated. But what is certain is that when we see Saul at the bottom of his spiritual crevasse, we'll be given the opportunity to step to the side and avoid falling into it ourselves.

I also wish I had better pastoral counsel for folks who have been injured by a Saul-like spouse, parent, or leader who abused their authority, got tangled up in sin, and started throwing spears. It would be great to have a simple, soul-soothing solution that elegantly explains how and why men and women of faith end up doing some really bad things. I'd like to have a clever little diagram with a couple of arrows and graphs so everyone would know why God-ordained leaders sometimes wind up being tormented by demonic powers and trying to kill those around them.

But I don't have a simple answer or a nifty diagram. So perhaps it would be best to start Saul's story at the beginning, to start our own trek to discover the spiritual roots of our own insecurities and sin right alongside Saul, on that very ordinary day when something extraordinary was about to happen.

Search Party

Overcoming spiritual insecurity involves remembering where we came from and how our spiritual journeys began

> *"Take now with you one of the servants and arise, go search for the donkeys"*
> *— 1 Samuel 9:3*

Saul's story begins down on the farm. He was the nearly forty-year-old son of a farmer who worked his family's land and did all the things that farmers have always done: plow, plant, and harvest. And when livestock got lost? He had to go looking for them. In the millennia before barbed wire and electric fences, lost and wandering livestock were a never-ending source of frustration for their owners.

So when Kish's donkeys went missing, his son was given the age-old chore of finding and bringing them back.

I don't know what to make of his father's word *arise*, but it's possible that the donkeys had gone missing the night before, and his old man came to him while he was still in bed. The mental image of a father getting his adult son out of bed to send him looking for some lost donkeys is a bit comical. But however it happened, Saul and his servant buddy put some serious miles between themselves and the home place the very first day. The Scriptures tell us "he passed through the hill country of Ephraim," which is about fifteen miles to the northeast of his hometown of Gibeah.

The fact that he is about forty years old when he pops up in the pages of Scripture is another curiosity in the puzzling life of Saul. The story of his ascension to the throne is not just a story about a common farmer becoming king, but it's also about a middle-aged man who receives an unlikely calling. Even though he was just half the age of Moses at the time of his calling, Saul was not a young man. A casual or cynical observer might diagnose Saul's wanderlust as little more than a normal precursor to a full-blown mid-life crisis. But with red sports cars still more than three thousand years in the offing, perhaps a week-long trip with a fun-loving employee would have to suffice.

I can almost see the gears in Saul's brain turning as he hatches his impromptu vacation plan. His father has told him to take one of the servants with him, so he runs a list of possible companions through his brain and then decides on the guy he knows will be up for a little fun along the way. I don't think there is an ancient Hebrew word for *road trip*, but it sure looks like Saul and his traveling buddy were thinking it as they threw their camping gear into saddle bags and hightailed off the farm before Kish changed his mind, or a neighbor came back with the missing animals.

That first night off the farm must have been fun, Saul and his buddy guffawing in the firelight, sipping from a skin of wine and eating the fresh snacks they would have packed for the trip. I can see them poking the fire, roasting kosher hot dogs on the end of sharpened sticks, telling stories, and loving every minute of the first night away from the dull routine. They try to stay up as late as they can to savor the moment, but their eyes grow heavy and they begin nodding off in the flickering light.

As Saul wriggles his oversized body into his bedroll, I can almost hear him thinking out loud to himself, "Yeah, this is just what the doctor ordered." He clasps his hands behind his head and takes in a deep breath and one long last look at the Milky Way shimmering in all its pre-industrial-age glory. He's a giant Jewish cowboy out on the range, contemplating the vastness of the universe as dreams begin to light up his mind. He smacks his lips and drops into an exhausted sleep after that first long day on the road.

Little does he know that the real search party has just begun.

Of course Farmer Saul, snoring under the stars, has no idea that his life is about to change in a way that no one could ever have imagined, that the creator of the galaxies that danced through the sky that night had already mapped out his destiny. In this way, Saul's story is just like ours. The next time you tell someone about the most significant moments of your life or listen to a friend tell about theirs, notice that nearly everyone's story starts out with words that say something like, "It was a day just like any other."

It's easy to read this story and not appreciate how very ordinary the first forty years of Saul's life must have been. No sooner do we read about lost livestock than we are swept up into the narrative of his miraculous encounter with the prophet Samuel, who anoints the unsuspecting farmer as the very first king of Israel. But for Saul and those around him, the day Kish's donkeys flew the coop was just another ordinary day.

The Lord certainly seems fond of calling farmers and shepherds into places of leadership. He put Adam in a garden. He called Moses when he was watching his father-in-law's herds. Even Jacob amassed a large flock of goats while working off his debt to his father-in-law. And David, Saul's successor, was from a farming family. The pre-industrial world was linked to the land in a way few of us are today. The simplest explanation as to why so many farmers and shepherds ended up in positions of leadership in Bible times is that nearly everyone was involved in producing their own food. The point is this: the Lord is fond of using regular people who do regular things.

To be sure, agriculture is not the only vocational pool that God is fond of calling people from. Paul was a lawyer, Matthew was a tax collector, and Peter was a fisherman. Yet people who know where their food comes from, who understand animals, soils, and seasons, seem well-suited for spiritual leadership. Even Jesus, who was a carpenter, used agricultural allusions and metaphors in much of his teachings because he lived in an age when virtually everyone, including himself, knew about things like weeds and sheep.

It should be no surprise, then, that when Saul the farmer became Saul the monarch, he could have felt pretty overwhelmed. For a guy who would have felt more at home in a barn than a palace to be called to be the king of a nation that had never had a king before is a pretty big deal, to say the least. I'm sure he must have been brushing his teeth some mornings and felt like pinching himself. It seems perfectly normal that he would have had serious self-doubts about his qualifications, and wondered about how a farmer could have the ability to accomplish the role of deliverer and protector of a nation.

I have some concerns that in the next age I'll have to meet Saul, that he'll call me onto the carpet of his celestial office and tell me to explain myself for writing this semi-biographical and speculative examination of his life and his insecurities. So just in case that happens, and on the off-chance he'll have a spear in his hand and not an angelic harp, I'd like to say, "Saul, I want to cut you some slack. For a guy who grew up on a farm and didn't have any role-model king to mentor you, you tried, you really tried."

If that meeting were ever to take place, one of the many questions I would like to ask him is why he packed all that food and traveled all those miles that first day, when all he was doing was looking for some lost donkeys. We'll never know for sure, but I have a few theories.

First, it's possible that those lost donkeys had a reputation for running fast and far, and the reason Saul and his servant packed enough food to last them for nearly a week and covered fifteen miles on the first day of their search was that those donkeys had escaped before and had been found in a far corner of the tribe's territory. Or maybe they thought someone stole those donkeys and would try to sell them in a place where no one would recognize the Kish family brand. But the animals are said to have been lost, not stolen, so that theory doesn't work well.

Perhaps there was a perfectly logical explanation for why Saul believed that finding them was going to take more than a couple of hours of asking around the nearby farms, or tacking up a few fliers with the donkeys' pictures on telephone poles in their neighborhood. But the little evidence we do have points us in a different direction.

The distance traveled the first day and the supply of food they packed don't make a lot of sense to anyone who has ever gone looking for lost livestock. Farm animals are usually recovered in some nearby greener pasture or consorting with others of their own kind, especially if it involves members of the opposite sex. I would tell you about my own experience of how our pigs broke out of their sty and ended up at our neighbor's barn about a mile away, socializing with their pigs. I would tell you about how difficult it is to herd pigs along a two-lane road while passing motorists waved and laughed. But I'm trying to forget that story, so I'm not going to tell it.

Which leads us back to suspecting that there were other things on Saul's mind when he set out on his search party. A more likely explanation is that Saul was like most anyone who has ever lived in a small town, or grew up tethered to a farm or ranch. That the lost donkeys were just a convenient opportunity for him to do a little wandering of his own, a good excuse to scratch the itch to get off the farm for a few days, a walkabout of sorts under the guise of a donkey recovery expedition. Even the circuitous route – a sixty-mile, five-day whirlwind tour of the land of Benjamin – leads us to believe that there is more to this excursion than just going out looking for some lost livestock.

It's likely that something else had started percolating in Saul's soul. Perhaps he was experiencing a God-given concern for the welfare of his depleted tribe, and he wanted to check in on them. Road trip, reconnaissance mission, or both – we'll never know for sure, but either way he wasted no time getting off the farm.

As his story unfolds, it is very easy to find fault with him. Easy to dissect his sins and insecurities and catalog his failings. Truth is, it's pretty easy to find fault with just about anyone who messed up as bad as he did. Later we'll have plenty of time to consider the traps he fell into, and try to learn from his mistakes. But like I said before, I want to cut him some slack.

So it would be good for us to take a moment and tip-toe up to Saul's campfire and spread out our sleeping bags next to his. To look into the night sky while we listen to his deep breathing, and the fire is still crackling and launching creamsicle-colored embers into the heavens. It would be good for us to consider how all of our lives are ordered by the wise providence of the Almighty, who both created the universe and calls us by name.

There are two things we can know for sure about Saul: The first is that he didn't set out that day to become the king; the second is that he didn't set out to make a complete disaster of his life. Like all of us who have ever had any inkling that God was calling us to a specific task or way of life, he started out with the best of intentions. Like Saul's, our journeys begin while we're looking for something other than the calling we've come to embrace.

It's healthy for our own souls to take the time to underscore that no one who gets into serious trouble, who ruins their career and family, starts out with the goal of ending up in such a desperate state. For the most part, we're all Sauls – regular people going about our everyday lives, doing everyday things, minding our own business – when God interrupts us.

For some, the interruption culminates with a dramatic event. This is how it was for Moses, who for forty years was doing nothing more than tending his father-in-law's flocks. Then one day that was just like the fourteen thousand or so other days before it, he saw a noncombustible bush burning on a mountainside, from which he heard the voice of God. For others, it's the head kick from heaven that knocks them to the ground, like King Saul's New Testament namesake experienced on the way to Damascus.

But regardless of how they end, our callings usually begin with something much more familiar. Like our tall friend sleeping next to us, we are just doing what we have done a hundred times before – looking for lost car keys, putting away the dishes, or starting up the stairs with a load of laundry – when we hear or see something that kindles something inside of us. A whisper in our inner being. We stand still for a couple of seconds and stare at nothing, while the tiny seed of an idea takes root in our imagination.

This is what I believe happened to Saul that day. Somewhere between the time his father told him, "Arise, go search" and when he and his buddy squealed the tires pulling out of the driveway, the seed of destiny dropped into his soul and germinated into the idea for a different kind of journey. The common seed of wanderlust found its way into the fertile soil of holy discontent in the heart of Saul. A Moses-like desire to go and look in on the affairs of his fellow tribesmen was taking root, so he packed enough gear to go explore some of the lands that he had never visited before. And maybe, just maybe, he might have a few funny stories to tell when he got back home and life returned to its predictable monotony.

If you've ever made a mess of things and ended up in a place you never intended, it's a good idea to remember how your journey began. If you've ever been terribly disappointed or injured by a leader, it might be good to think about where his or her journey started. It would have been good for Saul's soul to think back on the pedestrian beginnings of his journey, before his meteoric ascension to the throne and the dark days that later shrouded his soul. It would have been good for him to remember the road trip through the land of Benjamin, and how God took a donkey-chaser and made him a king.

Thoughts for Personal Reflection:

- Many of us have probably been injured by a leader who, like Saul, violated both moral and ethical boundaries. Have you ever considered how unintentional it was for those that fail in a significant way to get to that place?
- Do you think that your lack of success at an early age is causing you to doubt your ability to do something different today?
- Have you ever thought or believed that people should have special education or vocations in order to receive significant callings from God? If so, why?

Chapter 3

Insecure in the Word

Overcoming spiritual insecurity involves trusting in both the universal promises of Scripture that are for all believers and the personal promises and directives we receive from the Lord that are unique to us.

> *It shall be when these signs come to you, do for yourself what the occasion requires, for God is with you. And you shall go down before me to Gilgal; and behold, I will come down to you to offer burnt offerings and sacrifice peace offerings. You shall wait seven days until I come to you and show you what you should do.*
> *— 1 Samuel 10:7-8*

> *Now he waited seven days, according to the appointed time set by Samuel, but Samuel did not come to Gigal; and the people were scattering from him. So Saul said, "Bring to me the burnt offering and the peace offerings." And he offered the burnt offering...Samuel said to Saul, "You have acted foolishly; you have not kept the commandment of the Lord your God...But now your kingdom shall not endure. The Lord has sought out for Himself a man after His own heart..."*
> *— 1 Samuel 13:8ff*

Constructing a timeline for the first years of Saul's reign isn't simple, especially if one were to assume that all of Samuel's prophetic words to Saul were to be fulfilled immediately. If you happen to be a geeky student of the Bible like me, you may have already attempted to put together a timeline of Saul's encounter with the prophets, his coronation as king, the deliverance of Jabesh-gilead, his failure to wait the full seven days, not to mention everything else that happened in his life during that time. All these events take place in rapid succession. You will have already discovered, like I did, that you just can't make a timeline like that work without doing some real violence to the text.

When I first started to examine the life of Saul more closely, trying to compress all those prophesied events into a brief period of time felt like trying to stuff a queen-size mattress into a carry-on bag. Then I realized that Samuel gave us the timeline found in 1 Samuel 13:1 to let the reader know that the last part of his prophetic word to Saul, that he should wait seven days in Gilgal, was still some three years in the future.

I know that not everyone is interested in piecing together Bible timelines, and to be honest, I'm not usually interested in this kind of mental exercise either. But I think you'll come to agree that it will be worth the effort in this case, that we'll discover that the best way of sorting out the complexities of this passage underscores the truth that Biblical promises and prophetic words both have elements of immediate and future fulfillment.

For years I simply read this passage devotionally and didn't pay much attention to it chronologically. But as I became fascinated with the life of Saul and started looking closer at the geography and doing some simple arithmetic, it quickly became clear that the distances between the various locations, and the major discrepancies between the accounts of the events, meant that Samuel's prophetic instruction to Saul to wait seven days was still years away.

Some have suggested that the prophetic word that Saul would precede Samuel to Gilgal and wait seven days was fulfilled when he went there and was recognized as king by the entire nation, just after the spectacular victory over the Ammonites at Jabesh-gilead (1 Samuel 11:15). This explanation suggests that the prophetic seven-day wait that Saul failed to accomplish before the battle with the Philistines was actually a violation of a different and unrecorded prophecy given to Saul by Samuel at a different time. But there are at least two major weaknesses in this explanation.

First, Samuel tells Saul that he will offer both burnt offerings and peace offerings at Gilgal after the seven-day wait. In the account of Saul's national coronation at Gilgal, the text says that they offered peace offerings only; there is no mention of burnt offerings. This is no small omission. This is a time in history when even the minutest detail of sacrifice and offerings was meant to be scrupulously observed by the priest and prophets. We can be very certain that Samuel would not have left out something as important as burnt offerings being sacrificed at Saul's coronation.

The Hebrew word for burnt offering is *holocaust*, meaning "entire burnt offering." It was the prescribed sacrifice for the atonement of sin. The animal being sacrificed needed to be a male without defect, but most importantly the burnt offering required that the entire animal was to be burned up – no leftovers, and no part of it was ever to be used for food. This sacrifice occupied a unique place in the Jewish law (Leviticus 4:1-12).

The peace offering that Samuel records being offered at Saul's coronation was different. The animal sacrificed for a peace offering could be either male or female, and only portions of the animal's fat would be offered in the fire. The rest of the animal could then be used for food. Peace offerings were made during Saul's coronation. The meat from these animals made it possible for all those people to enjoy the celebratory feast as they ushered in what they hoped would be a time of peace and prosperity under the leadership of their tall, handsome, and courageous new king.

A second difficulty with understanding the coronation of Saul as the time of fulfillment of Samuel's prophecy is that the prophecy includes the information that Samuel would come and show Saul what to do. It points to a future time when Saul would not have clear direction, which fits perfectly into the context of the predicament he found himself in some three years later, when the Philistines were encircling his faltering army.

The conclusion to the first part of Samuel's prophecy reads, "Do for yourself what the occasion requires, for God is with you." This is a perfect description of the confidence and boldness with which Saul executed his duties as king during the first years of his reign. When Saul is coming back from plowing his fields, he gets the news about the desperate situation in Jabesh-gilead, and he knows exactly what to do. He immediately slaughters his oxen, cuts them into pieces, and sends their flesh throughout the territory of Israel to gather an army. Then after the victory, with great aplomb, he assuages the wrath of his most loyal followers, who want to punish the factions who initially rejected him as king. In a single stroke of monarchical genius, he both rescues a besieged city and unites the entire nation under his leadership. Bravo, Saul! Way to go!

Prophetic Understanding

You might be wondering why God would include a prophetic element whose fulfillment was still some three years away at this critical juncture in Saul's life. The simplest answer is that its fulfillment would require the development and maturation of all those character traits that God so values in all of us: humility, patience, and perhaps most importantly, continual dependency on Him. The rapid-fire, single-day, miraculous fulfillment of the prophetic word must have fired up Saul's soul like a shot of triple spiritual espresso. Yet God is not interested in shepherding a tribe of believers who can only function in the high-octane world of the immediate. He wants to be in relationship with us both in the moment of the miraculous and in those times when it looks like everyone and everything is falling apart, and all we can do is wait.

So, in my personal opinion, the best way of understanding this passage is to view it through the lens of the prophetic principle that is seen repeatedly throughout the Scriptures: specifically, that more often than not, prophecy has both immediate and delayed fulfillment. The fact that a prophecy is delayed does not invalidate it, nor does it release the one who received it from its mandates, or its promises and blessings.

A simple way to communicate this might be to read Samuel's prophecy with words of explanation in parentheses and italics that reflect the understanding of both Samuel and Saul when the word was given.

"And it shall be when these signs come to you, do for yourself what the occasion requires; For God is with you." (*Several years will pass, and then one day you will find yourself in a real jam where you don't know what to do. This is when you must remember the words of this prophecy.*) "And you shall go down before me to Gilgal and behold, I will come down to you to offer burnt offering and sacrifice peace offerings. You shall wait seven days until I come to you and show you what you should do."

Understanding the passage this way, as a prophecy with both an immediate and delayed fulfillment, also fits into the untimely nature of the prophetic in every age. I use the word *untimely* to say that prophecy rarely gets fulfilled in the time frame we want it to be. This is why the apostle Paul writes that "we know in part and prophesy in part" (1 Corinthians 13:9). And for the apostle Paul, this was not just doctrinal theory, but an experiential reality.

Saul of Tarsus (the apostle Paul's name before his conversion) had a very similar experience to that of his namesake, King Saul. Both of these Sauls from the the tribe of Benjamin received prophetic words that were not immediately fulfilled. Saul of Tarsus received prophetic revelation through Ananias immediately after his Damascus road experience that he would be a witness for Christ before kings, but the fulfillment didn't happen until some twenty years later, when after his arrest he preached to both kings and kingpins like Agrippa, Felix, Festus, and eventually even Caesar himself.

The fact that prophetic words don't always have instant resolution or fulfillment, and rarely have specific dates attached to them, should not discourage us. Remember that prophets see things in the here and now, and they also see things in the there and then.

Furthermore, prophetic words almost always place a certain level of responsibility on the person or group who receives them – responsibility to both obey and trust in such a way that the prophetic word will be fulfilled through the cooperation of the believer with the Spirit. King Saul's prophetic word specified that he would receive divine guidance after a seven-day wait. The guidance was God's part of the deal; waiting was his part of the deal.

Another New Testament example of this principle is the prophecy given by Agabus that predicted there would be a worldwide famine. Luke confirms that the famine happened during the reign of Claudius (Acts 11:28). In the very next verse, we learn that the church responded by taking up an offering to alleviate the suffering of the church in Judea (Acts 11:29). Forewarning the church of a massive famine was God's part of the deal; responding by gathering famine relief funds was the church's part.

Maybe you've never thought about how God invites us, even requires us to participate in the fulfillment of the prophetic. I heard a preacher say once that prophetic words were like long passes in a game of football. The player who wants to receive the pass must run to where the ball is going to be, not just stand idly by and assume that because it's a word of prophecy, it requires no effort on his part to fulfill it. Prophecies are meant to be run after.

Chances are, most of us, if not all of us, are in a very similar situation to Saul's. We have a promise from the Bible, or we have received a prophetic word that has not yet been fulfilled. Like King Saul, we are being asked to remember the prophecy and to do our part that it might be fulfilled. And sometimes, just like Saul, we are being asked to wait, and sometimes that wait is longer than we anticipated.

Saul's First Mistake

This is why the account of Saul's premature and inappropriate offerings of both the burnt offering and the peace offerings at Gigal is the beginning of the end for Saul's reign as king. It was his inability to trust the word of God when his success and reputation were on the line that uncovered his deep-seated insecurity in God's word to him. Biblical trust can be defined as obeying God's word in such a way that we will suffer real harm if God does not deliver what He promised us.

Saul's disobedience ensured that his reign would not continue into the next generation. He crossed the legitimate boundaries of his office and offered sacrifice, an act reserved exclusively for prophets and priests. He didn't wait the full seven days, but allowed his fear of failure to override his faith and trust in the prophetic words that were spoken over him some three years before.

By violating his God-given boundaries, Saul illustrates the truth that we'll never be asked to disobey God in order to accomplish His will. It might be tempting, but this is a great reminder that we only need to do our part – not someone else's, and certainly not God's. It can be especially easy to take it upon ourselves to do something or say something we shouldn't, when we already know God's will in a situation. It's tempting to want to help God and hurry things along. Certainly Saul knew it was God's will for Israel to live free from Philistine oppression, so when he saw his army falling away, he took it upon himself to keep it together.

It's also true that the more authority we have in any given situation, the easier it is for us to step out of our God-given limits in an effort to speed up the fulfillment of the prophetic word. I think it's fair to assume that if anyone other than Saul would have attempted to offer a sacrifice, the congregation would have stopped him dead in his tracks. But as king, Saul wielded authority that no one was willing to challenge.

David is a perfect contrast to Saul in this respect. David was anointed and received a prophetic word from Samuel that he would become the next king of Israel. But David never budged in his resolve to wait, and he was unwilling to kill Saul even when he had multiple opportunities to do so. For David, the prophetic word about becoming king didn't trump the sixth commandment not to commit murder. David stayed inside of God-given boundaries and waited for God to fulfill His word in His time.

David knew that God didn't need his help to make him king. He knew that he couldn't be both a lawbreaker and a fulfiller of prophetic promise. Apparently, God takes great pleasure in testing our integrity this way, because there always seems to be the opportunity to do similar things when He is the only one watching. He tests us to discover if we'll be like Saul and violate his word in a misguided and carnal attempt to accomplish His will, or be like David and wait.

Here are a few every day examples:

- The entrepreneur who has received a prophetic word that her business will be successful will undoubtedly be tested by opportunities to engage in less-than-ethical business practices.
- The single person who has received a word that she will find her mate may find herself tempted to cross boundaries in an attempt to secure someone's affections.
- The junior leader who has received a word that he will occupy a senior position in a church or organization may be tempted to speak ill of the current leader to accelerate a transition he feels is taking far too long.

I think I would feel far less frustration with Saul's disobedience if he had offered the sacrifice on the second or third day. But to have waited six days and twenty-something hours seems like such a waste. His last-minute collapse feels like losing a game in the third overtime by one point. This is a good thing to remember when we are waiting. Whether a little or a lot of time passes before a promise or prophecy is fulfilled, we don't have license to give up or do things ourselves. If we are going to walk in both the fulfillment and the blessings of Biblical promises and prophetic words, we will need to wait.

Jehoshaphat, another king of Israel, was in a situation not too different from Saul's about two hundred years later, when the nation was being threatened by foreign armies. This king humbly prayed, "We do not know what to do, but our eyes are on you" (2 Chronicles 20:12). Then a prophetic word came forth promising victory, and the king encouraged the people with these words: "Listen to me, O Judah and inhabitants of Jerusalem, put your trust in the Lord your God and you will be established. Put your trust in His prophets and succeed" (2 Chronicles 20:20).

All of us can be the recipients of accurate and powerful prophetic words, but we also have the potential, through disbelief and mistrust, to not act properly upon them. I'm glad we have both the negative example of Saul to teach us how not to respond to a prophetic word and the positive examples of Jehoshaphat and Paul to show us how to do it right.

Thoughts for Personal Reflection:

- What are some of the promises of God that you have trusted in?
- Are there specific things God has spoken to you personally concerning your future and your destiny?
- What things are you currently waiting for, and what are the temptations and distractions you've experienced during the wait?

Chapter 4

Power of the Spirit

Overcoming spiritual insecurity involves living in the Spirit

> *"Then the Spirit of the Lord will come upon you mightily, and you shall prophesy with them and be changed into another man."*
> *— 1 Samuel 10:6*

Saul had two powerful encounters with the Spirit of God. The first was just after he became king, and the second (which we will look at in more detail in the next section) was when he stripped off his clothes and lay naked in the presence of God. Both of these encounters were so extraordinary that the folks who witnessed them quoted the satirical proverb, "Is Saul also among the prophets?" because both events were accompanied by manifestations of the Spirit that appeared foolish and bizarre to those around him.

The first time the Spirit came upon him happened just after he was anointed as Israel's first king. Anyone who knew Saul would have been just as surprised as he was, not only at his selection as king, but also at his prophetic experience. Saul the farmer could have totally related to the prophet Amos's retort to Amaziah the rebellious king, when Amos told him,"I am not a prophet, nor am I the son of a prophet; for I am a herdsman and a grower of sycamore figs. But the Lord took me from following the flock and the Lord said to me, 'Go prophesy to My people Israel'" (Amos 7:14-15).

This is why the sight of the tall farmer who lived down the road being caught up in demonstrative, ecstatic religious revelry with a motley band of tambourine-banging, harp- and lyre-strumming, prophetic flautists must have gotten all the neighbors talking. They probably thought he had joined a cult. Yet transformative experiences with the Spirit are rarely decorous in any age. Saints have always been mocked. Revivals of all shapes and sizes always seem to come with enough odd-shaped baggage to make them easy marks for scoffers and skeptics. Whether it's Pentecostals rolling, Benedictines chanting, Baptists screaming, Methodists shouting, Quakers quaking, or Shakers shaking, every movement, sect, and denomination seems to have more than enough eccentricities to make its people stand out from the secular world around them, making them as easy to target as the broadest sides of the broadest barns.

My mom loved retelling the story of meeting two of my former classmates on the front porch of our family home. About ten years after graduation, two young women answered my mom's advertisement in the newspaper offering to give away the old upright piano she wanted to get rid of. After some chit-chat with my mom, the girls discovered that they were in the same graduating class as I was and asked her about what I had been doing since graduating. I assume they were expecting to hear that I was in prison, washing dishes at some dive on the Jersey shore, or just completing my third stint at rehab.

She told them that I was a pastor and that my wife and I had started a church in upstate New York. This is when they laughed in her face. Both of them, as my mom loved to tell, simultaneously broke into uncontrollable laughter when they heard this most improbable story. They had known me in high school and hadn't heard that I, like Saul and Amos, had had an encounter with the Holy Spirit that neither they nor I ever saw coming.

The move of the Spirit is never comprehensible to the natural mind in any generation. Whether it's old classmates, coworkers, or the neighbors down the road, it's unlikely they will understand what has happened to those who have been set apart for the Gospel. It's why the Bible says, "The natural person does not accept the things of the Spirit of God, for they are folly to him and he is not able to understand them because they are spiritually discerned" (2 Corinthians 2:14).

Was Saul among the prophets? Heck yeah he was, and he needed to be. If there was ever a man who needed a touch from the Holy Spirit, it was Saul. His undersized identity banging around in that oversized body needed more than the status quo brand of generic religion that had left the nation of Israel internally fragmented, spiritually depleted, and under constant assault from its enemies. Saul, with insecurities sweating out of every pore, was in critical need of the Spirit of God coming on him and enabling him to accomplish the things he would never be able to do himself.

Sadly for Saul, his family, and his nation, the anointing and power that fell upon him that day was just a temporary experience rather than an ongoing lifestyle.

It's easy to be dismissive of ecstatic religious experiences when those experiences don't bring lasting change to the character of the person who has experienced them. I think the first time we hear the refrain asking, "Is Saul among the prophets?" there was a genuine amazement that he was part of that seemingly eccentric group of men. The second time we hear the refrain, it's easy to hear the cynics' intonations. After all, by now everyone knew that Saul had become a murderous sovereign bent on exacting ruthless revenge on anyone who stood in his way, and the fact that he was hanging around with the prophets just made the whole situation seem even more pathetic.

Before Jesus, the Spirit of God temporarily rested upon humans, empowering only a few special souls for specific tasks and limited seasons. Since the resurrection of Jesus, the Spirit indwells all believers, an indwelling made possible by the atoning work of Christ. Normal people, farmers, and even punks from New Jersey now experience even more fully what only prophets, priests, and kings occasionally experienced long ago.

Unfortunately, believers can fall into a pattern similar to the one Saul exhibited: having temporary, non-transformative experiences. We attend church or special meetings where we experience the move and power of the Spirit, but resist the experience of His deep indwelling. We can neglect the indwelling of the Spirit and seek to replace that experience with external ones. My friend Nita calls folks who fall into this error fire truck believers because they chase after the fire and smoke of revival like firemen on their way to a five-alarm blaze. Like Saul, we can find ourselves participating in the outpourings of the Spirit while neglecting the cultivation of a daily experience with Him.

Please don't misunderstand my thoughts to mean that I'm against revival or outpouring. I just want to remind all of us that these events and manifestations are simply part of the Christian life, and were never meant to be a substitute for the security of having a regular, personal indwelling experience with the Lord.

Thoughts for Personal Reflection:

- How do you cultivate the daily presence of God in your life?
- How have outpourings affected you or those around you?
- Have you ever seen things in a spiritual setting that seemed bizarre?

CHAPTER 5

Insecure Position

OVERCOMING SPIRITUAL INSECURITY INVOLVES FINDING OUR IDENTITIES APART FROM TITLES, OFFICES, AND POSITIONS

> *Now the Lord said to Samuel, "How long will you grieve over Saul, since I have rejected him from being king over Israel?"*
> *— 1 Samuel 16:1a*

> *He proceeded there to Naioth in Ramah; and the Spirit of God came upon him also, so that he went along prophesying continually until he came to Naioth in Ramah. He also stripped off his clothes, and he too prophesied before Samuel and lay down naked all that day and all that night. Therefore they say, "Is Saul also among the prophets?"*
> *— 1 Samuel 19:23-24*

Every four years the following oath is taken on January 20th in Washington, D.C.:

> "I do solemnly swear (or affirm) that I will faithfully execute the Office of President of the United States, and will to the best of my ability, preserve, protect and defend the Constitution of the United States."

Before someone can serve as president of the United States of America, he or she is sworn into office on inauguration day. If you've ever watched the ceremony on TV or been there in person, you know it's a who's who of important people. Supreme Court justices, members of the House of Representatives, senators, celebrities, everybody who is anybody in government is usually in attendance. But perhaps what is most amazing is that our military is involved in the ceremony.

It's amazing because the peaceful transfer of power happens every four years, and for the most part Americans (and nations with similar governments) take it for granted. It's like, ho hum, we have a new president. Our military leaders recognize the new president, or the same person if he or she has been re-elected, who by virtue of the office becomes their new Commander-in-Chief. They salute him when he walks by and carry out his orders when he gives them.

But a quick glance at the news shows us that the transfer of power in other countries is often anything but peaceful. It seems like every week we read or hear about a new coup d'état or revolution, or learn that members of an opposition party have been rounded up and imprisoned, or that former leaders have fled their country. We see the riots, disappearances, and assassinations in places where the side with the most guns and muscle determines who is going to rule the country.

This is precisely what happened in the nation of Israel because Saul was unable to voluntarily accept his demotion. His unwillingness to voluntarily abdicate his throne resulted in decades of unnecessary violence and bloodshed that nearly ripped the nation apart.

Two things were at work in Saul in those years between God's demotion of him and his death. The first was his inability to discover and accept his identity apart from his office. The second was his inability or unwillingness to act upon the message God was trying to communicate to him by the Spirit. If Saul could have acted on either of these, things would have been so much better for the nation, for his family, and for him.

Rejected as King

At first glance, the rejection of Saul as king sure looks like God's rejection of Saul the man. But the text is very clear; read it again if necessary. God rejected him as king. God did not reject Saul as a person.

The fact that God did not reject him is evidenced by what may have been as many as twenty years between David's anointing as king and Saul's and his sons' deaths. During those years the tender mercies of God were patiently working like a team of skilled surgeons operating to separate conjoined twins. God wanted to separate the entwined identities of Saul the person and Saul the king. Tragically, he resisted the Spirit's leading to surrender his position and was killed by Philistine archers who targeted his royal robes.

This inability to accept and embrace our identities apart from our positions, titles, and gifting is at the very core of how our personal insecurities can impede the advancement of the Kingdom of God. Our inability to accept change and let go of a role or office is often rooted in an abiding sense that being a child of God is not enough. Perhaps we're afraid of what will be seen when everything is stripped away and we appear before the One "to whom all things are open and laid bare to the eyes of Him with whom we have to do" (Hebrews 4:13).

It's fair to say that all of us appreciate, and even need, some amount of encouragement and approbation from those around us. I can't imagine going through life without some applause and cheering from my friends and family, and I want to be part of a family and community where we regularly encourage and root for one another. Heartfelt and honest praise is a good thing... to a point.

The problem arises when our need for external validation, the applause or affirmation that our roles and positions afford us, becomes a substitute for the security of knowing that being a child of God is enough. Whether or not our desire for approbation has reached an unhealthy level can be measured by our willingness to lay aside a position or role.

A friend of mine tells the story of when he was leading a small church that was in the process of bringing on a new pastor. During a meeting with the congregation a few weeks before the new pastor was to arrive, he told everyone that when the new pastor did come, no one's job, title, or role in the church was guaranteed, even his own. He emphasized that if the new pastor thought someone should be retired from a role or moved into a new one, then that's the way it would be. Nearly everyone nodded their heads in agreement with this excellent advice. Unfortunately, as you might have predicted, some of the members really bristled at the suggestion that they would lose their office or ministry. One high-profile leader even went so far as to tell everyone in the meeting that he would never leave his position!

Of course, as you probably have already guessed, that brother went through a pretty traumatic ordeal as he was eventually separated from the title he had come to love. Like the boy goaded into licking the frozen flag pole, we find our skin stuck in such a fashion that pulling away is going to cause some pain. It's really easy to have our skin stuck on the sweet taste of titles and position. All of us should be wary of getting to a place where our affection for a title or the pleasure of functioning in a certain role becomes a surrogate for God's acceptance and love for us.

When left unattended and unpruned, this kind of entanglement of our positions and our identities is way more critical than a stuck tongue. It can be likened to a cancerous tumor whose roots and tentacles become entwined in a major organ. The kind of tumor that the surgeons can't remove because it has become so much a part of the organ that simply cutting it away would kill the patient. Likening our love for a title or position to a tumor is pretty radical, but make no mistake about it – it can be just as deadly.

It's all too easy to convince ourselves that everything we're doing meets with God's approval because He is using us and blessing us in some public role. But this becomes a potentially deadly trap when our position behind the microphone or in the inner circle of decision-makers becomes a surrogate for the unmerited love of God. This is a toxic source of affirmation that replaces the affirmation we get from our identities as children of God. A good first step in making sure we never get to such a dangerous place would be to recognize that the very things God has called us to do have the real potential to become dangerously entangled in our identities.

Operating under the anointing feels good. I heard a teacher say that the anointing travels along the same neurological pathways that sex does. I don't know if he was right about that, but ministry sure seems to have the ability to energize and affirm us in a way that few other experiences can. It can appeal to our sense of vanity and lead us to believe the illusion that because we hold a position or operate in a gifting, God has placed His stamp of approval on everything we do and say. We can only imagine how intensely satisfying and pleasurable all of this must have been for Saul – leading troops into battle to punish injustice, restoring honor and and glory to his tribe, plus all the perks and privileges of monarchy. I'm glad I'll never have to deal with all the success and power he did: his nearly absolute power that could buy or take whatever distraction his starving soul craved, the opioids of power and pleasure that can temporarily distract us from our real need and momentarily quiet the spiritual cravings that only an abiding connection with the Lord can sate.

It's scary when we realize that Saul's transformation from benevolent king to malevolent despot happened almost overnight and early in his reign, when he discovered he could leverage his position as the king of the first authentic theocratic monarchy the world had ever known. The privileges of his position could numb the pain of his personal and family shame, and the bevy of sycophants and hangers-on would have applauded his every decision and catered to his every whim in hopes of having some favor bestowed on them. His inaccurate self-assessment and persistent lack of confidence could be hidden behind the satiny folds of his royal vestments and buried under all the pomp and circumstance his office afforded. Saul became a skin-and-bones believer hidden under the baggy robes of monarchy.

We will say it again. God was not rejecting Saul, He was rejecting him as king. Saul's mistake is that he interpreted God's rejection of him from his position as God's complete rejection of him as a person. Just because God fired him from being king doesn't mean God was firing him from being His child. This part of Saul's story reminds me of a conversation my friend Justin had with the Lord just after the birth of his first son.

On the night he and his wife brought their son home from the hospital, Justin was on the back steps of his apartment smoking one of those "It's a Boy" cigars with the blue wrappers that new dads are so fond of handing out to friends and coworkers. This is when the Lord asked:

"Do you love that boy?"

"Yeah God, totally, of course."

Justin was wondering why God was asking him such a silly question with such an obvious answer. Then the Lord said:

"I feel the same way about you. Before you could talk, before you could walk, before you could do anything for yourself or for me, I totally loved you."

Who knows, maybe even the angels are puffing away on cheap cigars every time a child of God comes home. But regardless of how they celebrate, it's good for us to know that there is a world of difference between being rejected and being relieved of one's position. The problem, of course, is that, like Saul, most of us have a really difficult time not taking a demotion or a change in position personally. Like Saul, we have the ability to hide our thin spirits behind the microphones, titles, and guitars, and find ourselves in a place where who we are and what we do become all tangled up.

This is another one of those crossroads in Scripture where we would do well to slow down and imagine what a different ending there could have been for Saul and his family. If he would have gracefully accepted his demotion and taken his place as an ally and supporter of the new king, this choice could have led him back to a place where he could have experienced joy as a child of God apart from his achievements and title.

Naked Spirituality

In the second passage at the beginning of this section, we find this odd story about King Saul getting naked after the Spirit came upon him. He stripped off all his clothes and lay in his birthday suit in the presence of Samuel and the prophets for a day and a night. But this was not just a one-man burlesque show, or the story of a sovereign streaking onto the field at halftime; this was a dynamic encounter with the Spirit and yet another missed opportunity for Saul to voluntarily resign as king.

The disrobing of Saul was a perfect response to the Spirit of God. For years prior to this event, God was trying to get Saul to take off his royal robes and surrender his position voluntarily. It was the very thing that the Spirit of God prompted Saul to do when he prophesied naked before Samuel. For about twenty-four hours Saul was exactly how God wanted him: naked. Just like Adam was in the garden and Jesus was on the cross.

Adam frolicked around paradise with his unclothed bride in a world before shame. Jesus was stripped before they put him on the cross, and He crucified humanity's shame that rested on his bloody body. Saul's nakedness was a prophetic pantomime; he was acting out in the Spirit the very thing God wanted him to do in the natural. It was as if God was saying, "Saul, I love you. I see the real you – you can't hide behind all those fancy frocks, shiny armor, and royal robes. I want you to be in a place where you're not hiding anything from me; you can come naked to me, and I love you."

Sadly, Saul put his clothes back on. We don't have any information about what happened when this spiritual episode ended. Perhaps he fell asleep and awoke in the morning and only then realized he was naked. Perhaps he awoke to the voices of those around him who were making sport of him and picking up the taunting refrain, "Is Saul also among the prophets?"

I can almost see Saul the morning after. He's lying on the floor between two rows of pews, but for a moment he can't figure out where he is. All he knows is that he feels good and that he's slept better than he has in years. He yawns, rubs his eyes, and stretches his arms as far as they will reach. But then he hears some whispering and snickering and opens his eyes to see a few young men looking at him from the corner. Perplexed but unfazed, he scratches his side, then starts to scratch himself a bit lower. He sits up in an instant and looks down at his unclothed flesh. He gives the guys in the corner a quick look, and they head for the door. He snaps his fingers and his valet runs to bring him his clothes. Later that day while traveling back, he informs his staff that if even one word of this incident finds its way out, they'll all be very, very sorry. This is how I imagine him slamming shut the door on what might have been his best opportunity to abdicate his throne and fully embrace the next season of his life.

Thoughts for Personal Reflection:

- Do you believe that God loved you before you could do anything?
- How has your calling affected your relationship with God?
- If you were asked to resign your position today, how do you think that would impact your relationship with God?

CHAPTER 6

Psalmsless Saul

OVERCOMING SPIRITUAL INSECURITY INVOLVES CONNECTING WITH GOD REGULARLY ON A PERSONAL LEVEL

> *So it came about whenever the evil spirit from God came to Saul, David would take the harp and play it with his hand; and Saul would be refreshed and be well, and the evil spirit would depart from him.... Now it came about on the next day that an evil spirit from God came mightily upon Saul, and he raved in the midst of the house, while David was playing the harp with his hands, as usual; and a spear was in Saul's hand. Saul hurled the spear for he thought, "I will pin David to the wall." But David escaped from his presence twice.*
>
> *— 1 Samuel 16:23, 18:10-11*

Two of the first three kings of Israel were singer-songwriters. David composed his Psalms, and Solomon wrote the Song of All Songs, but Saul has no songs to his credit. This doesn't mean that Saul didn't try to write songs or poems; it's possible his stuff just wasn't very good, or he was too insecure to let others hear it. Or perhaps he went to an open mic night at a local cafe and didn't get enough applause, or got heckled by a drunk. Even the most gifted and creative can be sent into an emotional tailspin by bad reviews, and it does seem like musicians, writers, actors, and most creative people are particularly sensitive to criticism and are often plagued by some fairly intense insecurity.

I also imagine it's pretty difficult to do much composing when your pen is a seven-foot spear, and your harp is a javelin. This passage of Scripture tells us that David was always carrying his harp, and Saul was always packing his spear. Note how the text draws attention to what was in each man's hand, and sandwiched between is the phrase *as usual*, or as the original Hebrew says, "day by day." We all keep things handy and hold onto the things that are important to us. Smart phones. Purses. We're like the basketball-obsessed kid who carries the ball to class and dribbles it down the street.

To David, music was the most important thing. We know this to be so because we have his last words, in which he describes himself as "the sweet psalmist of Israel" (2 Samuel 23:1). Of all of David's titles and achievements, this is his description of himself on his death bed. At the core of his being, David saw himself not as a warrior or a king, but as a psalmist. So very different than the last words of Saul, which begin with the gruesome request, "Draw your sword and pierce me through with it, lest these uncircumcised come and pierce me through and make sport of me" (1 Samuel 31:4).

Musical worship is an important part of every believer's spiritual life. This is evidenced by how passionate and particular most believers are when it comes to the kind of music that is used for worship. Normally mild-mannered saints can become downright ornery when the style of music changes in their house of worship. And while I've never known of a worship leader, other than David, who actually had to dodge an assassination attempt while worshiping, just about every worship leader I've ever known has had all kinds of comments, critiques, and criticisms thrown at them by unhappy saints who are not fond of the new playlist.

I don't think there is anything more to say about the merits of traditional worship music over more contemporary styles, or vice versa. But I do have a theory about why many believers are so passionate about their music, a passion that is present regardless of whether the music was birthed three hundred years ago by a hymnologist with impeccable theology, or birthed three months ago by a new believer strumming on an untuned guitar. The reason is nostalgia. We can couch the discussion in all kinds of misappropriated Bible verses or apocryphal anecdotes about the influence of music on a particular sect or people group, but the core issue is that we all love the music that was in our ears when we first fell in love with Jesus.

Believers are like couples who have what they call "our song." Sometimes it's the song that was on the radio when they first fogged up the windows of their dad's car. It's the music that the worship leader was singing when you first responded to an altar call, or got on your knees and recommitted yourself to following Jesus. There is nothing to be ashamed of or feel guilty about; we all love the music that reminds us of our first days of being close to the someone we love, even the Lord.

If you were to spend any time with me gardening or on a construction site, you would quickly discover that I become like a jukebox of thirty-year-old worship tunes. I know it drives some people crazy to hear me sing. I'm tone deaf and have almost no musical sensibilities; nonetheless, I love making melody in my heart, and out of that abundance, my mouth spews fragments of twisted lyrics and off-key melodies.

Thankfully, I think I've finally gotten past the place where I'm willing to throw down my gloves and start fighting about the style of music folks prefer. All I care about is that it is passionate and sincere. Apparently, the Lord feels the same way about music, because He chose not to include the musical scores that were used to accompany any of the songs found in the Bible. We have the lyrics and some historical notations about accompaniment and structure, but no music. My thought is that if the Lord wanted us to sing and dance in a particular style, He would have included the sheet music along with the Psalms, hymns, and spiritual songs that we have all through the Scriptures.

Songs Of Deliverance

While we don't know the melodies and beats of the music David used to serenade Saul, we do know that David's worship music was apparently the last thing Saul clung to as his spiritual life was failing, because it had the power to temporarily evict the evil spirit that was afflicting him. As Saul's connection with God became ever weaker, he required the services of a spiritual surrogate, and so David became his living, breathing iPod. David was recruited for his gifting in musical worship long before his military and leadership skills were evident, and his harp and his voice were his ticket from the pasture to the palace.

Music is unique in both its power and its appeal, and the Psalms of David are perhaps the most powerful and appealing music of all. It is as if the Psalms were extruded from David, songs wrung out from a place so near the core of his being that the lyrics are as close as anyone has ever gotten to what I would call the universal essence of mankind. Trials, temptations, tribulations – you name it, David experienced it. And all those hardships squeezed his spirit, soul, body, and relationships until he vented them in song.

He was in so much pain that he just had to let it out. Even the groaning too deep for words that Paul writes about often seems to come from a place of pain. Reading the Psalms makes me feel like I'm reading the transcripts of some prisoner who was tortured for secret information or a confession of guilt. I suppose we all feel like prisoners under the interrogator's lash sometimes.

Yet I'm thankful David's vent was his writer's tablet, and all generations since have nodded their heads and said to themselves, "Yeah, that's how I feel" when they hear the words that erupted from the unseen core of his soul. The ability to put words and images to universally recognizable experiences and emotions is what makes poetry, music, literature, preaching, and all art, for that matter, truly great.

I'm so grateful David had the courage and spiritual security to spill into print what he was really feeling, without having to filter his words through some kind of religious censorship obsessed with pasting a cheery, churchy face on every facet of the often painful experiences that are part of all of our lives. His lyrics are definitely not the stuff of the bumper-sticker theology of our age that often trivializes the Christian life.

This is why I love David as portrayed in the Rembrandt picture *Saul and David.* If you take a moment to look at the painting, you'll see the face of a young man totally caught up in musical worship, completely oblivious to the machinations of the demonized king who is drying his tears with the other side of the curtain. It's easy to imagine Saul nodding his head in intuitive agreement when a lyric plucked a common chord in his heart as David sung his early Psalms.

Saul's relationship with David reminds me of the lyrics of Roberta Flack's old hit song:

> Strumming my pain with his fingers
> Singing my life with his words
> Killing me softly with his song
> Killing me softly, with his song
> Telling my whole life with his words
> Killing me softly, with his song

Killing me softly with His Psalms. Killing me softly with His words.

This is the ultimate purpose of all Scripture: the invitation to come and die to ourselves. But death rarely comes easy. We gasp for our last breath. The God-given instinct for survival extends to our souls, where it drives us to defend our positions and dominate those around us. Yet musical worship has the power to euthanize our soulish desires and selfish ambitions.

Poor Saul. He missed the whole point of worship music. He

would find himself in a spiritual funk and call for David to come sing and play. But the music for him was little more than a spiritual bong. He inhaled its vapors, and it dulled the pain. But with every passing day of rebellion and disobedience, the music lost its potency. Eventually, the same worship music that had the power to displace demons became the prelude to the attempted murder of the worship leader.

Worship fixes a lot of things, but it won't fix rebellion and disobedience. If we're stealing from our employer or gossiping about our neighbor, no amount of worship is going to remedy that. Sure, we might feel better for the hour or two we are in the presence of God, but make no mistake about it – we can soon find ourselves throwing spears just like Saul.

Thoughts for Personal Reflection:

- Do you worship when you are alone?
- Why do you think worshiping in a group is a different experience than private worship?
- Have you ever tried to use music to soothe your feelings of guilt or shame?

CHAPTER 7

The Wicked Witch

OVERCOMING SPIRITUAL INSECURITY INVOLVES EXCLUSIVE DEVOTION TO THE GOD OF THE BIBLE

> *Then Saul said to his servants, "Seek for me a woman who is a medium, that I may go to her and inquire of her." And his servants said to him, "Behold, there is a woman who is a medium at En-dor."*
> *— 1 Samuel 28:7*

> *So Saul died for his trespass which he committed against the Lord, because of the word of the Lord which he did not keep; and also because he asked counsel of a medium, making inquiry of it and did not inquire of the Lord. Therefore He killed him and turned the kingdom to David the son of Jesse.*
> *— 1 Chronicles 10:13-14*

Following Saul as he goes into the witch's house is the scariest part of his whole story.

Personally, I don't even watch horror movies, and I stay clear of anything spooky or that gives me the willies. Meditating and thoughtfully examining this darkest time in Saul's spiritual life makes me want to flip the page as soon as possible, so we're going to spend as little time as we can in her house.

It's safe to assume that from the outside, the witch's house would have looked the same as every other house on the block. Saul himself had outlawed sorcery from Israel years before and made it a capital offense, so she wouldn't have had a neon sign out front advertising palm and tarot card reading. Even her front room would have been swept of any evidence of her business, lest a door-to-door peddler or nosy neighbor catch a glimpse of some incriminating paraphernalia in the living room.

When Saul comes knocking at her door to inquire about her services, she leaves the door chained and pretends not to know a thing about that sort of business, and even reminds the potential client of the illegality of what he is looking for. He assures her that no harm will befall her, and even swears to God that she will not be punished. She looks the tall man up and down, and eyeballs the two fireplugs standing behind him. It doesn't take a medium to know who the big hunk being tailed by guys wearing sunglasses and earbuds really is, so she lets them in.

Stepping across that threshold seals Saul's fate. He might just as well be an over-aged trick-or-treater lured into the house of a serial killer. Like an ox to the slaughter, he follows when she motions for him to come into her back room. A shadowy room where thick curtains are drawn, and the walls are covered with ghoulish knickknacks and fetishes. She dons a shaman's shawl and begins her incantations. Soon she is lost in the waves of the netherworld, rocking back and forth while conjuring the images of the dead that she is paid to consult. She shrieks so loudly that the bodyguards peek into the room to see if their boss is okay. But Saul seems fine, except that he's apparently talking to someone they can't see.

Saul hears the voice from the dead telling him that he and his sons will be with him the very next day. With this, Saul collapses and sprawls on the floor. He's too weakened from his fasting and too traumatized by hearing his unappealable death sentence to get up. The witch and Saul's men eventually coax him to eat what was perhaps his last meal. After they eat, they slip out of the house and into the night to return to the encampment to await the dawn of the king's final day.

Whether the witch really FaceTimed Samuel from the dead doesn't matter at this point. Perhaps she was just a charlatan, as some have suggested, because the word *En-dor* means "ventriloquist." Or maybe it wasn't Samuel who came and rebuked Saul from the grave, but just a demonic apparition. Or maybe it really is an account of a successful seance. We'll never know, and it doesn't matter because he was killed for inquiring. Like I said, it's a scary story.

There are several practical lessons we can take from the witch's house, but that is all we'll take. Everything else should remain untouched, and don't even think about taking home any souvenirs from her place!

The first lesson is that God is concerned about our intentions, whether they be for good or evil. Saul was judged because he inquired. The judgment had nothing to do with whether or not the witch had authentic spiritual abilities. The pursuit of spiritual counsel apart from God is the issue. In the same way that the witch was not fooled by Saul's disguise, God is not fooled by our pretending to be getting a cup of coffee when what we're really doing is trying to overhear what our coworkers are gossiping about.

Another lesson is that he changed his clothes. If you have to disguise or hide yourself to do something, it's probably a bad idea. And unless we're a secret Santa or planning a surprise birthday party, thoughts or sentences that start with the words "I don't want my parents/wife/husband/church friends to know" are almost always going to end poorly for us.

A third lesson is that very few things remain hidden. Saul went out of his way to keep his visit secret, but now we and the billions of other people who have read the Bible know all about his not-so-secret rendezvous with the medium. And he was outed without the help of hidden cameras, private investigators, or IP addresses. But getting busted is not the worst thing; getting away with this kind of activity is much worse. This is why one of the consistent manifestations of grace in the life of the believer is getting found out before more damage is done.

The final thing we should take from the witch's house is the knowledge that we are never going to find security in our relationship with God if we keep jumping from god to God to god. In the same way, we're never going to experience relational security if we practice jumping from person to person. The first commandment will always be the first commandment: that we are to have no other gods before Him.

Thoughts for Personal Reflection:

- Have you ever owned something that seemed to have spiritual power?
- Have you ever visited a fortune teller, and if so, what did you experience?
- Have you ever considered why the first commandment is the first commandment?

SECTION III:
The Insecure Spouse

Chapter 8

The Insecure Spouse

So David and Abishai came to the people by night, and behold, Saul lay sleeping inside the circle of the camp with his spear stuck in the ground at his head; and Abner and the people were lying around him.
— 1 Samuel 26:7

And the name of Saul's wife was Ahinoam the daughter of Ahimaaz.
— 1 Samuel 14:50a

"Dearly beloved, we are gathered here today in the sight of God and the face of this company, to join together this Man and this Woman in holy Matrimony..."

The singsong voice of the old minister rises and falls like the head of a carousel horse.

"...which is an honorable estate, instituted of God in the time of man's innocence..."

His enormous eyebrows look like wooly batons moving with the beat of the liturgy.

"...let him now speak, or else forever hold his peace..."

He delivers his lines flawlessly, while thinking about the open bar, whether the girl is already pregnant, and the width of the envelope the father of the bride will slip him during the reception.

"Do you, Saul, take Ahinoam to be your lawfully wedded wife?"

The big question rolls off his tongue like a spoonful of clover-blossom honey. He lifts his palms to the heavens so his robes unfurl like the gilded wings of an enormous purple butterfly. He pauses with a tilted head and listening ear, and raises those eyebrows impossibly high, as a climactic cue for the groom to give his hearty "I do."

But there's no answer. Only silence. A murmur rolls through the synagogue.

The cleric turns his head and flashes a coffee-stained smile. He glares at the groom who stands dazed and mute before him. The minister clears his throat for all to hear and asks the question a second time. He lowers his voice and turns up the volume, clipping the end of each name. After all, he's the ecclesial maestro who's been brought in from out of town to officiate the big day, and there can be no slip-ups when he's officiating.

"DO YOU, SAUL, TAKE AHINOAM TO BE YOUR LAWFULLY WEDDED WIFE?"

The words hang in the air like black-bottomed clouds on a muggy afternoon. Ahinoam's tiny hand squeezes Saul's giant mitt. He blinks, looks at his bride, and starts mumbling.

"I do...well...err... I'm pretty sure I do. Oh, I don't know. Ahinoam, do you really love me? I mean, you're sure about this, right?"

But the old pro has heard enough and cuts Saul off in mid-mumble, and nearly shouting, proclaims:

"AND NOW BY THE AUTHORITY GRANTED TO ME BY THE LORD GOD OF ISRAEL AND THE STATE OF BENJAMIN, I PRONOUNCE YOU HUSBAND AND WIFE. SAUL, YOU MAY KISS YOUR BRIDE."

The congregation lets out a collective sigh; a tambourine starts jangling while young men whistle and old women daub their eyes. Ahinoam is saying something, but Saul can't hear her because the wedding party has descended upon them, and the newlyweds are swept up in the tide of revelers who have come to get the party started.

The boom of the DJ's oversized woofers starts to throb, and a disco ball is shooting streaks of starry light pinwheeling across the hundreds of smiling faces of friends and family. Meanwhile, out in the entryway, a bartender is dropping olives into a second tumbler for the preacher who just snatched the marriage ceremony from the flames.

After the father-daughter dance, while the best man slurs his way through his toast, Saul and Ahinoam catch each other's eyes. Saul looks away. Ahinoam bites her lip. It's going to be a long marriage, and soon Saul will be sleeping with his spear.

I'm sure you realize by now that this is not how Saul and Ahinoam's marriage actually began. Everyone knows that disco balls weren't invented until about the third century, and woofers weren't used in weddings until the Middle Ages. But I'm hoping a playful look at Saul and Ahinoam's wedding day might help us start thinking about how our own insecurities could be undermining our marriages and romantic relationships.

Insecurity in romantic relationships is the squeakiest wheel on the insecurity wagon. It's possible that you've skipped ahead to this section because your marriage, engagement, or romantic interest is in serious trouble. You might suspect, or someone has suggested, that your or your partner's insecurities are in large measure the source of ongoing skirmishes, arguments, and interpersonal drama that seem to be a never-ending component of your relationship.

Regardless of the age in which we live or the customs of our cultures, insecurities in romantic relationships are among the easiest of all to see. Intense jealously, control issues, and the demand for non-stop communication and affirmation are just a few of the relation-eroding behaviors of someone who is too insecure to enjoy a healthy and satisfying romantic relationship, let alone a marriage.

Or perhaps you're currently single, and you've come to suspect that your insecurities have sabotaged previous relationships or scared off prospective mates. That insecurity hangs around your neck like a sachet of garlic, an abiding sense of being unlovable and unworthy of love. It fogs the atmosphere around you and makes it all but impossible for a potential mate to find you.

So a desire for a quick fix is completely understandable. The stress and heartache of a rocky romance is enough to get almost everyone searching for a solution. Unfortunately, there are few, if any quick fixes for insecurities, including the relational insecurities – the ones that erupt like cold sores on the morning of the wedding. Yes, those insecurities.

Oh, that there were a quick cure, a lovey-dovey potion we could sprinkle on our sick relationships and make them all better. Or perhaps an elixir we could drink, so everyone could love and be loved until death do us part. If we could bottle a remedy for romantic insecurity, we'd all be billionaires.

What we do have in abundance is the endless stream of relationship advice from so-called experts, who peddle their multi-step snake oil solutions for romance and their recipes for relational bliss on talk shows and bookstore shelves. Glasses of ideas, tablespoons of psychotherapy, pinches of spicy stories all whisked together into drinks that are celebrity-endorsed and PhD-recommended. We knock them back one after the other and hope it will fix both us and our partners.

But pounding those cocktails doesn't heal our relational insecurities any more than acne cream heals heart disease. The misappropriated feelings that compel us to behave insecurely in our relationships are far more invasive and deeply rooted than we usually realize. So for most of us, God's curative power for our relationships will come upon us incrementally, as we grow into our new identities and gather strength in the security of His embrace. Ultimately, the curse of relational insecurities will only be broken as our souls find a security that's even more compelling than the warmth of a secure, exclusive, and loving relationship with our spouse.

Sexual shame, opposite-sex approval, body image, and ungoverned sexuality are just a few of the possible sources of the relational insecurities that we see manifested in Saul. The Scriptures give us several tantalizing glimpses of Israel's first royal couple that should help us understand how our insecurities might be sabotaging our own relationships. And while ancient Hebrew weddings and marriages weren't the same as ours, we know just enough about Saul and Ahinoam to see the peaks of their relational mountains poking through the clouds of history, a few images that will help us understand how insecurities were sabotaging Saul's marriage. Sorry, no disco ball and no woofers. But maybe just enough clues to help us on our journey to break the curse of insecurity that is undermining our own romantic relationships.

Chapter 9

Sexual Shame

Overcoming relational insecurity involves coming to terms with our personal and family sexual shame

> *"Am I not a Benjamite, of the smallest of the tribes of Israel, and my family the least of the families of the tribe of Benjamin? Why then do you speak to me in this way?"*
> *— 1 Samuel 9:21*

The tribe of Benjamin had a reputation.

It was at the center of one of the most shameful sex scandals of the entire Bible: a same-sex, lust-fueled gang rape and murder that culminated in the near annihilation of the entire tribe during a brief and bloody civil war.

When Saul reminds Samuel that his tribe is the smallest, he is telling the truth. The few generations since the war that had brought his tribe to the edge of extinction were not enough time to repopulate their numbers. What is even more interesting is that Saul says that his individual family is the least of this smallest tribe. His words deserve a closer look; they point to the possibility that his family in particular had the worst reputation in a disreputable tribe.

But before we look at Saul's family specifically, lets take a moment to understand the scandal and its aftermath. The account is found in the last three chapters of the book of Judges. Feel free to read the entire account at some point as part of your personal study, but for now let me give you a thumbnail account of the events at the root of the sexual shame fueling some of Saul's profound insecurities. Quite possibly, this same kind of shame is fueling some of ours.

The story begins with a Levite whose significant other cheats on him and leaves.

Throughout the passage you'll see that Levite referred to as the woman's husband, but she is called a concubine and is never named. In Bible times, women who lived with men without being married were often known as concubines. They were lovers, mistresses, and baby makers, but relegated to a second-class status. They had some of the benefits and protections afforded a wife, but for reasons of social order, ethnicity, or convenience, these women were not considered eligible for full legal marriage. They were not entitled to inheritance, family name, and other protections under the law, and as we will soon see, they were often victims in that hyper-patriarchal culture.

The story begins with the woman going back to live at her father's home in Bethlehem, and four months later the lonely Levite shows up in an attempt to patch things up. The Scriptures say that he went to "speak tenderly to her in order to bring her back" (Judges 19:3). After he spends nearly a week at his fathers-in-law's home, she either agrees or is compelled to return with him. On the day they depart, the couple gets a late start. They don't leave until after lunch, and they make it only as far as the town of Gibeah, about eight miles away.

According to the custom of the day, they went to the center of town with the expectation that they would be taken in for the night by a local resident. Even today, Near Eastern cultures highly value the virtue of hospitality, so when the Levite and his concubine find themselves without a host family after sundown, it is a harbinger of darker things to come.

A little later, an old man who was not a Benjamite is on his way home from work and finds the travelers alone in the town square. Surprised by his adopted community's lack of hospitality, he brings them into his home and cares for both them and their animals. They are enjoying a pleasant evening together when they are interrupted by pounding at the door.

The old man goes to the door to discover that a crowd of men has surrounded his house. The mob is demanding that the Levite be handed over to them so they can have sex with the traveling cleric. He pleads with them to abandon what he calls "wickedness and folly," and in a desperate attempt to appease the mob, he offers up his own daughter as a victim. But the men are not interested in the girl; they remain fixed on raping the Levite.

In a final attempt to appease the mob, and presumably to escape being gang raped himself, the Levite grabs his concubine and pushes her out of the house and shuts the door behind her. The sex-crazed men pounce on the woman and abuse her all through the night. In the morning her husband opens the door and finds his concubine barely alive. She soon dies, and the Levite drapes her lifeless body over his donkey and goes home.

Then the Levite cuts his concubine's body into twelve pieces.

He sends a body part to each corner of the nation, a macabre call to arms to avenge the brutal rape and murder. They gather in the city of Mizpah to agree on a course of action and assemble an army. First they send envoys into the territory of Benjamin to demand that the rapists and murderers be surrendered to them for justice.

But the tribe of Benjamin is having none of it. Instead of surrendering their kinsmen, they gather their own army and prepare for war.

What ensues is a brief and bloody civil war that kills some forty thousand men of Israel, leaving only a band of six hundred men of Benjamin alive. The survivors escape into the wilderness and find refuge at a place called the rock of Rimmon, and for the next four months, the unprotected land of Benjamin is razed by the armies of Israel. Women and children are murdered and the cities burned to the ground, while the surviving bachelor soldiers languish in exile.

Afterward, the nation experiences regret over the genocide and impending extinction of the defeated and humiliated tribe. They want to provide wives for the six hundred survivors so the tribe can be repopulated. But there is a problem. Before the war, the nation took a solemn oath forbidding anyone to give their daughter in marriage to any Benjamite. This, in effect, sentences the surviving six hundred to a lifetime of involuntary celibacy. Unable to break their vow, the men of Israel devise a diabolical two-fold solution to maneuver around the issue.

First, they raid the city of Jabesh-gilead. This city is selected because it had not sent a delegation to the mustering of troops at Mizpah. The only people spared in the raids are young virgins, who are abducted and given to the surviving Benjamites as wives. But there are not enough of these orphan brides to go around; there are still two hundred more Benjamite bachelors in need of wives. This is when the nation of Israel gets really creative.

They decide to orchestrate the illusion of a *mass kidnapping* of two hundred single women at an annual dance festival held in Shiloh. The bachelors of Benjamin are instructed to hide in the vineyards and catch their wives as they dance past them during the festival. (We've italicized the words *mass kidnapping* to draw attention to the fact that the most likely scenario for what happened at the festival was more like a mass opportunity for families to marry off their unwed daughters, who would have gone to the festival knowing they would be kidnapped.)

With some forty thousand casualties in the civil war with Benjamin, the entire nation of Israel would have been experiencing a shortage of eligible men. The dance festival charade would not only provide husbands for single women, but also give their families the plausible deniability they needed to avoid being found guilty as oath-breakers for voluntarily allowing their daughters to intermarry with the blacklisted Benjamites.

This is how the tribe of Benjamin was nearly exterminated and then repopulated.

And you thought your family had some crazy history and dark secrets.

The sordid history of the tribe of Benjamin goes a long way toward explaining Saul's surprise at being selected as Israel's first king, especially in light of the fact that these horrific events were still relatively fresh in the minds of the people. But perhaps even more telling is that Saul finds it necessary to remind Samuel of the unworthiness of his family in particular – that not only is the tribe of Benjamin the smallest, but that his family is the least in the smallest tribe.

The Least

Saul's word choice is very curious. The Hebrew word translated *least* is used in other places in the Old Testament to convey the idea of the youngest, or the least significant and worthy of honor. Because Samuel traces Saul's family tree back six generations, it's safe to say that Saul's family was not the youngest family in the tribe, and every family in the tribe could trace its ancestry back to one of the six hundred survivors.

Saul must have used this word for *least* in the other sense: "least worthy."

I believe that Saul considered his family the least worthy because his family was at the very center of the scandal. Saul and the rest of his tribe knew that the ugliest skeletons were hung in the Kish family closet, and those dark events were still casting a shadow over Saul and his clan when Samuel first spoke to him about being chosen as the first king of Israel. The evidence for this is convincing. We know that Saul's home town of Gibeah was the place where the scandal occurred. With only six hundred men from the entire tribe escaping into the wilderness, only a handful of them would have been from the town of Gibeah. So here is what I think happened.

In the aftermath of the tragic and vile events described in the book of Judges, the rumor mill would have undoubtedly started to churn out the names of the men who were most to blame for the tribe's destruction and humiliation. Pinning blame has been part of the human experience since Adam tried to throw Eve under the bus in Eden, so in the wake of such a disastrous series of events, finger-pointing within the tribe would have been inevitable.

The tribal leaders who were unwilling to surrender the guilty men would have been targets in this blame-fixing for sure. But the primary targets would have been the men of Gibeah, the ones who were part of the original homosexual mob who raped the concubine to death. We'll never know exactly what role Saul's ancestors had in that crime, but because they were from the town of Gibeah, and because there were so few survivors of the civil war, it's highly probable that Saul's ancestors were at or near the center of the scandal.

This is why Saul's confession that his family was the least seems very much in line with the behavior of someone who is afflicted by a profound and abiding sense of shame, the kind of opprobrium that can be explained by knowing that your not-too-distant ancestors were perverted, violent, and willing to go to war rather than let their family members face justice.

Sexual immorality, and the shame associated with it, seems to have the unique ability to cling to the psyche of the human soul more tenaciously than almost any other class of sin or behavior. This is why the apostle Paul reminds the Corinthians to "[f]lee immorality. Every other sin that a man commits is outside the body, but the immoral man sins against his own body" (1 Corinthians 6:18). Sexual sins affect us in a unique way.

This kind of shame would have been especially potent for the nation of Israel, which retained the clear moral mandates of the Old Testament. Laws prohibiting adultery, fornication, homosexuality, and all other forms of sexual practice outside of marriage. The destruction of the cities of Sodom and Gomorrah was initiated by a very similar assault by a homosexual mob desiring to rape the angelic visitors to Lot's home. This account is found in Genesis, the same book of the Bible that establishes the identity of the nation of Israel. Make no mistake about it, the sin of Gibeah was a clear violation of their foundational laws.

If Saul's ancestors were camel thieves or ran a Ponzi scheme, I doubt Saul would have been plagued by such a deep sense of shame over his family's reputation. Today, sexual sin does not generally carry the weight it once did. Yet sex crimes still carry a stigma and a level of shame that puts them into a class all by themselves. Even in prisons, where thieves and murderers abound, the men who have perpetrated sexual crimes, especially against children, are segregated from the general prison population because they are so often the victims of violence at the hands of other prisoners who despise them.

Gay Debauchery

The narrative of the book of Judges makes it clear that the mob that eventually raped and murdered the Levite's concubine wanted to have sex with the Levite. We can attempt to manipulate the text or exegete away the Biblical explanation of the mob's desire to have "relations with him," but any fair-minded reader with even a basic understanding of Hebrew understands that this mob is acting upon a kind of homosexual frenzy. This is why the old man who is hosting the Levite says, "Do not act so wickedly, do not commit this act of folly" (Judges 19:23). Without doubt, Saul, Samuel, and the rest of the nation knew many of the specifics of both his tribe's and his family's crimes.

Nonetheless, it's remarkable that the same nation that so zealously pursued justice and then revenge from Saul's ancestors for their sex crimes seemed so unfazed and blind to all the other sexual sin and barbarism that preceded and followed. Examples of the injustices so readily accepted in that era include the Levite's illegitimate relationship with a concubine, a culture of misogyny, the hospitable old man's willingness to offer up his own daughter to the sex-crazed mob, the Levite's sacrifice of his concubine to the mob, the genocide against Benjamin, the annihilation of the innocent population of the city of Jabesh-gilead, and the kidnapping of four hundred virgins and their involuntary marriages.

The double standards of that age have nothing on the double standards of this age. Yet in spite of all the sin, the men of Gibeah were still considered the worst of the worst and found themselves consigned to the very bottom of the bottom of the moral barrel.

I hope this account will shed some light on one of Satan's most effective gambits: That is, to lure people into behaviors that are so repugnant and so vile that we come to believe there is no possible forgiveness and redemption. He attempts to brand the human psyche with an indelible mark, a permanent tattoo, a scar of shame – call it what you will. For Saul and the rest of the tribe of Benjamin, the story of a homosexual mob intent on raping a Levitical priest is exactly the kind of shame that can keep a man or woman from accepting and receiving forgiveness.

All this guilt and shame was compounded by the tribe's institutional endorsement of the crime, demonstrated by their unwillingness to bring the individuals responsible to justice. Whenever institutions, families, or individuals participate in the cover-up of similar sinful and/or criminal behaviors, they simply compound the shame of victims and multiply the inevitable consequences.

Here are the final two reasons I'm convinced that sexual shame was a primary factor in Saul's profound insecurities. The instant he learned that the city of Jabesh-gilead had been besieged, he leapt into action. Considering that more than half of his tribe was directly related to the orphaned brides kidnapped there, this seems logical, but it also sent a clear message of his tribe's identification with the city that was on the fringes of the nation's borders.

The second reason is even more convincing. He cuts the oxen into twelve pieces and sends them throughout the nation. This action was a bloody reminder that the twelve pieces of the butchered concubine sent to the nation was a call to arms. There is an irony here; no, much more than irony. It's a stab at redemption. It was a grizzly reminder, a flesh-and-blood reenactment sent in the mail to remind the nation of its own sin in that tragic civil war, and the opportunity to make amends to the city it razed.

Sending the twelve pieces of oxen was a kind of sacred theater, a sort of ancient holy performance art that elegantly communicated both his tribe's ownership of their sin and the beautiful depths of God's forgiveness and acceptance. Forgiveness and acceptance demonstrated by God's sovereign choice of a man from the smallest tribe and the least worthy family to be the first king of Israel.

God is fond of going to the dregs to find his servants. He's not squeamish about plunging His holy hand into the filth of human frailty and taking hold of the raunchy and rancid. God went to the bottom of the last barrel to choose the first king of the nation of Israel.

This is why the called-of-God, men and women like Saul, often experience such bewilderment and surprise when they are chosen in spite of sketchy pedigrees and personal histories. Why, even the apostle Paul echoes his namesake's surprise and bewilderment at being chosen of God by saying, "For I am the least of the apostles, and not fit to be called an apostle, because I persecuted the church of God" (1 Corinthians 15:9).

And the apostle reminded the church in Corinth:

> "For consider your calling, brethren, that there were not many wise according to the flesh, not many mighty, not many noble; but God has chosen the foolish things of the world to shame the wise, and God has chosen the weak things of the world to shame the things which are strong, and the base things of the world and the despised God has chosen, the things that are not, so that He may nullify the things that are, so that no man may boast before God. But by His doing you are in Christ Jesus, who became to us wisdom from God, and righteousness and sanctification, and redemption, so just as it is written, *'Let him who boasts, boast in the Lord.'*" (1 Corinthians 1:26-31, emphasis mine)

Thoughts for Personal Reflection:

- Why do you think sexual shame carries with it a stigma different than that associated with other sins?
- How do you think sexual shame manifests in marriage?
- Do you think past behaviors can disqualify someone from certain roles and vocations?

Chapter 10

Opposite-Sex Approval

Overcoming relational insecurities involves accepting our sexual identities apart from illicit sexual experiences and inappropriate affirmation

It happened as they were coming, when David returned from killing the Philistine, that the women came out of all the cities of Israel, singing and dancing to meet King Saul, with tambourines, with joy and with musical instruments. And the women sang as they played, and said,

"Saul has slain his thousands,
And David his ten thousands."
— 1 Samuel 18:6-7

It was a girl band that made the song "David Has Slain His Ten Thousands" a number-one hit during the reign of Saul. Two times in this passage, Samuel makes sure the reader knows that it was a group of women who were leading the victory parade back to the palace after the nation's big win over the Philistines, banging on their tambourines and singing and dancing. It's easy to imagine their smiling faces and colorful dresses whirling down Main Street. Ancient Israel's cheerleaders were strutting their stuff for their kingdom, and you can be sure all the men were checking them out.

Men want the approval of women. Women want the approval of men.

Humanity is hardwired with an acute awareness of what members of the opposite sex think of them, and Saul was no exception to this. Somewhere in all of us is something of the first couple's lost innocence that craves the admiration and applause of the opposite sex. A desire to stand naked in front of another human being and feel no shame.

We don't have the musical score to this song, but it must have been catchy, because it was being sung all the way across the border in the land of the Philistines. It was this song that the military advisers of Achish, king of Gath, used to convince him that David was not to be trusted. My assumption is that this song was still ringing in Saul's ears when he awoke the next day, the first day he tried to kill David. I think if a boy band had sung the song that day, the outcome would still have been the same. But at this critical juncture in Saul's life, it was the sound of women's voices that drove him from simple jealously to murderous envy, and their song was the straw that broke his swaybacked soul.

A conversation about sexual approval is a good prelude to a broader discussion about sexual identities in general. Sexual identity issues evoke powerful emotions, and they are still hotly debated today. They are considered by many to be as foundational to personhood as ethnicity, and governments are passing legislation that recognizes a citizen's self-identification to be the ultimate arbiter of sexual identity.

Abuse and exploitation often occur when the desire for approval is sexualized, and this can lead to catastrophic consequences for the most vulnerable, from the preteen girl who discovers that older boys will pay attention to her if she is sexually active, to the young man so desperate for masculine approval that he becomes the target of older homosexual men who groom him for sex with expensive gifts, personal attention, and affirmation.

For Saul, the virile and fertile heterosexual, being number two on Ancient Israel's Sexiest Man of the Nation list was not an option. Apparently, fathering no less than eight children with two women was not enough affirmation of his manhood. This is one of the curious phenomena about sex: more of it does not necessarily make us happier, nor does it fix the deeper issues that drive our behaviors.

Piling up sexual encounters in an attempt to establish or maintain our identities reminds me of how cities and towns along the shores of the Great Lakes get rid of excess snow after a blizzard. The snow is cleared from streets and bridges by heavy equipment and loaded onto tandem-axle dump trucks, then hauled to the lakes, where it is slid off into the icy water. In the wake of a big storm, tens of thousands of loads are dumped in the lakes, and giant mounds of snow pile up around the wharfs and bulwarks. But before too long, the giant snowbergs begin to melt away into the waves. No matter how many million cubic tons of snow are dumped into the water, the water always wins.

The inexorable melting-away of experiences, like snow in the water, seems to capture a bit of the futility of trying to solve a sexual identity issue by the accumulation of sexual experiences. Like all insecurities, it's the dog that can't be fed and the itch that can never be scratched. The attempt to establish one's identity from the skin in points to the real issue – that of not being secure and content in one's own sexual identity and God-given boundaries.

Because we don't have any specific details about Saul's and Ahinoam's domestic life, we'll never know if she even attempted to give him the approval and acceptance he so desperately needed. My suspicion is that she tried for a while, and then gave up once she realized how hopeless it was.

It would also be silly for us to imagine that their ancient domestic life resembled our modern images of a healthy and monogamous marriage. It might be entertaining to imagine Saul and Ahinoam as the stars of a vintage television series where each episode begins as Saul wheels his chariot into the driveway and comes through the door announcing, "Honey I'm home," while hanging his armor in the hallway closet after a hard day at the palace. It's fun to imagine Ahinoam's shy smile when Saul comes into the kitchen, slips his big hands around her waist, gives her a peck on the neck, and asks, "What's for dinner? I'm starving," and their three bright-eyed kids come bounding in from the backyard. But it would probably be best if we change the channel and leave the image of them spooning in front of the stove for another age.

A better use for our imaginations would be to visualize how much more fulfilling and different our own relationships would be if we sought to discover our sexual identities apart from both experience and the approving nods or askance looks of others. As you already know, the great ambition of this book is to encourage all of us to behave just a bit less insecurely. So I don't have any expectations that these few words about sexual identity will solve anyone's sexual identity dilemmas. But hopefully these words and thoughts will get the conversation started, and most importantly get the conversation started between you and God, because I believe the issue of sexual identity is so perplexing that only God Himself can sort it out for us.

If this issue is something you're dealing with, my primary pastoral counsel to you would be to simply remind you that ultimately this is a you-and-God thing. It is very unlikely that a person or even a community will ever be able to adequately address these difficult issues for you. At best, sexuality is complicated, so when we mix sin into the equation, things become really confusing. A first step would be to abstain from sexual sin and let the unmasked pain and discomfort of holiness reveal some of the deeper core issues that drive your appetites. My only other piece of advice would be to encourage you to deal gently with yourself.

Thoughts for Personal Reflection:

- In your opinion, how do sexual identities differ from ethnicity?
- Do you think having a long list of lovers and sexual experiences increases or decreases our sexual insecurities?

Chapter 11

Anorexic Soul

Overcoming relational insecurities involves accepting an accurate self-image

"He had a son whose name was Saul, a choice and handsome man, and there was not a more handsome person than he among the sons of Israel; from his shoulders and up he was taller than any of the people.
— 1 Samuel 9:2

Therefore they inquired further of the Lord, "Has the man come here yet?" So the Lord said, "Behold, he is hiding himself by the baggage."
— 1 Samuel 10:22

"Is it not true, though you were little in your own eyes, you were made the head of the tribes of Israel? And the Lord anointed you king over Israel..."
— 1 Samuel 15:17

Anorexia nervosa is an eating disorder. Those suffering from it have an irrational fear of becoming obese, so they starve themselves and become unhealthily thin. Yet regardless of their actual weight or their famished appearance, they believe they are fat. And no matter how much family and friends try to convince them that they are too skinny and plead with them to eat more, they continue to see themselves as needing to lose a few more pounds. In spite of protruding hip bones, sallow complexions, and gaunt cheeks, anorexics look into the mirror and see something completely different. Their self-perception is so distorted that they have lost touch with reality, and so they don't see a starving person; they actually see an overweight person.

Apparently Saul shared an anorexic-like detachment from reality. His profoundly insecure soul distorted his self-perception like a fun house mirror bends and twists an image. If we were walking with Saul in the mall, and all of us us stood in front of a mirrored storefront, I believe he would have seen something different than the rest of us saw. We would see a tall, handsome man, and he would see a small, unappealing man. He would see a man unworthy and unable to assume the office of king, while we would be looking at a guy who looks like he was born for the job.

But Saul lived thousands of years before anything like the mirrors we have today first appeared. There were no family photographs and no selfies to look at. All he had were the shadowy images reflected back by ancient mirrors made of polished metal, or perhaps an occasional glimpse of himself in a pool of still water when he knelt down to drink. Like all the ancients, he didn't have a way to see himself as he really was. But even if he had our reflective technology, it probably wouldn't have made a difference.

The essence of insecurity is an inaccurate view of ourselves. It causes us to both undervalue and overvalue things, and it twists our ability to accurately appraise what we are really worth. We don't know why he had this inaccurate understanding of himself, but we do have the authority of Scripture and God's own commentary on Saul's self-image: "You were little in your own eyes." This is not the diagnosis of Saul's psychiatrist, pastor, or family counselor; it's the opinion of the Almighty.

This divine summary statement of Saul's self-image extended beyond his psyche and soul. It encompassed how he understood his physical appearance also. This goes a long way toward explaining how someone of his physical stature thought he could hide in the luggage on the day of his coronation.

Likening insecurity to anorexia might just be the most precise way that I know to think about the subject. A conversation about a distorted self-image could easily be inserted into a discussion about any facet of insecurity, because it depicts the phenomenon of how our insecurities skew and bend our self-perception. To be sure, a bent and twisted self-image has a negative influence on every sphere of our lives, but its most profound impact might well be in the area of courtship and marriage, the most intimate of all human relationships, where how we look and how we see ourselves has a direct impact on whom we kiss.

Over the years, any number of studies and experiments have been conducted showing how appearance affects the way people treat each other. Not that we need studies, experiments, and hidden cameras to prove what most of us have intuitively known since elementary school: namely, that the tall and the good-looking are treated better than those born with average height and looks.

In one study, scientists had college students look at photographs of different men in a controlled setting, and asked them to choose the men in the pictures who they thought were best suited for leadership.[1] The students chose taller men far more often than their shorter counterparts. This bias explains why American presidents are taller than the average American man.

Another spin on our concern with appearance involved a television news program that hired two actresses to stand next to a stranded car along a busy road. They each stood beside the same exact car, and each one wore the exact same outfit. The only difference was that one of the gals was average looking, and the other was a knockout. Can you predict what happened? Of course you can. All those knights with shining tool boxes apparently see pretty clearly through their visors.

In a similar experiment, women were asked to choose potential mates from different men standing in a police-like line-up behind a one-way mirror. The results were the same. Women chose taller men time after time, even when the shorter men were given fabulous resumés that included great wealth or prestigious careers.[2] Sorry, ladies, even your gender isn't above being influenced by appearance.

And let's remember that even the most spiritual people can be influenced by looks. It was the prophet Samuel himself, the one who anointed Saul as king, who thought David's tall, handsome brother Eliab was the shoo-in replacement for the tall, handsome Saul. This is when the Lord had to remind Samuel that God looks at the heart, not the body (1 Samuel 16:6-7). So let's not assume our spirituality automatically exempts us from this powerful and universal human bias.

Can you imagine what people saw and felt when Saul walked into the room? Women would start fanning themselves, and politicos would start scheming. Yeah, Saul had it all. He was the son of a mighty man, the best-looking guy in the nation, and a full head taller than his peers. He was the kind of guy that political parties would swoon over today. With his nation in the market for its very first king, Saul seemed to have been born at exactly the right time, and he came of age at the juncture in Israel's political history when the nation was looking for a leader who really looked the part.

---

[1] Fleming, Nic. "Voters View Tall People as Better Suited for Leadership." *The Guardian*, 18 Oct. 2011, https://www.theguardian.com/science/2011/oct/18/voters-tall-politicians-leadership. Accessed 28 Jun. 2018.

[2] Stossel, John. "The Ugly Truth About Beauty." *ABC News*, 23 Aug. 2002, https://abcnews.go.com/2020/story?id=123853&page=1. Accessed 28 Jun. 2018.

But isn't it puzzling that the folks like Saul, with the best looks and the best physiques, don't always feel as secure as one might think they would? Beautiful people, athletic people, super-talented and famous people often suffer from intense insecurities about their appearances, oftentimes even more intensely than the rest of us. This is how it was for Saul. He was a GQ cover guy, yet felt compelled to stuff his oversized body behind the suitcases on the day he got the crown put on his head.

But Saul is anything but unique in this sense. If you're anything like me, you don't always like the way you look in photos. Like many guys my age, I look a bit like an overinflated pool toy, and while I'm really happy about having two eyes and two ears, I'm not quite as thrilled about having two chins. Don't misunderstand me, I'm not suggesting that our appearances are supposed to be a primary issue in our romantic relationships. I just want us to be honest about the fact that we all judge by appearance, or at the very least, are influenced by the way people look. This is why I think it's fair to say that insecurities revolving around body image can profoundly impact our romantic relationships.

An accurate understanding and correct valuation of our worth is going to be part of the process of becoming free from the curse of self-doubt and the fears that fuel our sometimes irresistible urge to act on these feelings. But make no mistake about it – Saul's mistakenly low view of himself did not disqualify him from being selected as Israel's first king. Quite possibly, the opposite was actually going on. Perhaps it was his humility and childlike bewilderment in response to his royal calling that endeared him to God and made him the best choice. But somewhere along the way, this inaccurate view of himself began to steer him in the wrong direction. Like an oar dangling over the side of a row boat, the drag of an inaccurate view of himself pulled him off course.

To be sure, most humans undervalue themselves; the human soul seems predisposed to harsh self-judgment and low self-esteem. But it's equally, or possibly even more dangerous to think more of ourselves than we ought. This is why Paul warned the saints in Rome "not to think of [themselves] more highly than [they] ought to think" (Romans 12:3). The enemy of our souls is content with dragging us off course with the dangling oar of an inaccurate self-image on either side of our boats.

I absolutely believe that an accurate-enough self-image is attainable in this life, on the condition that we remain humble and teachable. I have personally experienced the Spirit of God bringing regular course corrections to my self-image and perceptions that have kept me heading in the right direction. But an accurate-enough self-image is so very different then a perfect self-image, which we are never going to have on this side of eternity. Even the nearly perfect mirrors of a space telescope can't give us that kind of reflection.

It's disquieting when we come to accept that we will never have a perfect self-image. But once accepted, this truth leaves us with a craving for the next age, in which believers will enter into a different realm, and the out-of-focus image of ourselves will be brought into balance by our face-to-face encounter with the resurrected Christ. We can hear the longing for this consummation in the words of Paul when he writes, "For now we see in a mirror dimly, but then face to face; now I know in part, but then I shall know fully just as I also have been fully known" (1 Corinthians 13:12).

Thoughts for Personal Reflection:

- Why don't we post unflattering pictures of ourselves on social media?
- In your opinion, how much focus on personal appearance is appropriate?
- What do you think is the biggest obstacle to accepting our own appearances?

Chapter 12

Circumcision Of Sexuality

Overcoming our relational insecurities involves letting God control our sexual behaviors

> *"This is My covenant, which you shall keep, between Me and you and your descendants after you: every male among you shall be circumcised. And you shall be circumcised in the flesh of your foreskin, and it shall be the sign of the covenant between Me and you."*
> *— Genesis 17:10-11*

Saul was a Jewish man, and like all Jewish men, he would have been circumcised when he was eight days old. His father, or another trusted man known as a *mohel*, would have performed the ceremonial surgery, the removal of the male child's foreskin. Circumcision was and is the primary marker of God's covenant with the Jewish people. Today the ceremony is called a *bris* or *brit-milah*, and after the surgery there is a big meal and party, welcoming another boy into the Jewish community.

Perhaps you have never spent much time thinking about why God chose circumcision as the sign of covenant and as a way of distinguishing the Jewish people from the rest of the world. But it is one of those Biblical curiosities that has perplexed me because, at first glance, circumcision does not make a lot of sense. If I wanted to give a group of people a distinguishing mark, a way for everyone to know who was part of the group and who was not, circumcision does not seem like a very good choice for a few obvious reasons.

First, it only marks one half of the population. Only males are circumcised, so women are completely left out of this covenantal rite. It's the historic marker of God's covenant with his people but only applies to men. Like I said, it doesn't make much sense to me.

Second, it's not readily visible. Unless you're skinny-dipping with your buddies or in the locker room showers, you're not going to know whether a man has been circumcised or not. I think a facial tattoo or some other kind of visible permanent scarring of the face would make more sense.

I also wonder if the early Christians who were trying to enforce Jewish law in the church, especially about circumcision, were willing to take a guy's word for it? Legalists are not very trusting in general, and so I assume they would have conducted some kind of inspection in the men's room just to make sure. Conducting penis inspections at church seems absurd, but it underscores the apparent mystery of cutting off the skin at the end of a man's penis as a sign of covenant.

This takes us to our final point. Doesn't it seem more than just a little odd that the same God who designed and created the human body with a protective shroud of skin over the most sensitive part of the male anatomy would then command His chosen people to cut off said part of His creation? Think about it: Jewish men were forbidden to cut off even their sideburns, and hair grows back! But amputation is permanent, and the surgical removal of human flesh seems downright barbaric, if not foolish, to the natural observer. Unless it points to something far more significant – which of course it does, because God chose this small operation to make a big point.

Men highly value their genitals. Duh. No big revelation here. But the fact is, most men would choose death over castration and/or penile amputation, and we have evidence of this from history.

During the second world war, a land mine developed by the Germans was given the euphemistic nickname "Bouncing Betty" by American troops. The German army buried millions of these mines, and some historians believe it to have been one of the most effective weapons of the entire war. It was a simple device, consisting of a metal canister containing hundreds of metal balls and two explosive charges. When the footfall of an advancing soldier triggered the mine, it ignited the first small charge that lifted the canister a few feet into the air; then the primary charge detonated, spraying the area with a waist-high cloud of those metal balls. As you've already guessed, the power of this weapon wasn't that it killed effectively, but that it paralyzed troops with fear. The same young men who were willing to risk their lives charging machine gun positions found themselves completely immobilized by the possibility of being emasculated by one of these terror mines.

The high value men place on their anatomy is exactly why God chose circumcision as the primary marker for covenant. It's a symbolic surgery signifying the fact that He has rightful authority over our reproductive rights, sexual identities, and sexual behaviors.

The permanent scarring of the male anatomy, the part of the

body that is the most difficult to govern, was the perfect marker of covenant before Christ. Circumcision is an ancient symbol for the spiritual truth that if we are going to be in covenant with God in any age, then we must be willing to relinquish authority over everything, even the proverbial family jewels.

Since the death, burial, and resurrection of Jesus Christ, circumcision is an optional surgery with zero spiritual value, and attaching spiritual significance to circumcision is a wrongheaded understanding of the Gospel. But this does not change the fact that He has the rightful authority to expect us to bring every aspect of our lives under His control. It also serves to remind us that no external law or rite will ever successfully govern our sexuality. In this way, perhaps circumcision can be seen like the points of the compass chiseled into granite by a mapmaker from a previous age. A cut in the ancient rock of man's flesh, pointing humanity to a time when the Spirit of God would empower them to accept His rightful authority to govern their sexuality. Having one's sexuality governed and regulated by God is one of the greatest miracles in all of human experience.

Rizpah Promiscuity Porn

In addition to his wife, Saul had a concubine, and her name was Rizpah. It's worth mentioning that the name Rizpah means "coal" or "hot stone." Saul, it seems, was attracted to a hottie. The fact that she was an exceptionally attractive woman seems to be confirmed by the fact that his military general Abner started cavorting with her soon after Saul was killed in battle (2 Samuel 3:7).

Saul was circumcised in the flesh; of this we can be sure. But he and most of the men of the Old Testament did not have their sexuality consistently governed by God. Extramarital sex and polygamy were the norm in Bible times. Even among the patriarchs and heroes of the faith, monogamy was the exception and not the rule. Sure, they were circumcised in the flesh, but their sexuality was often way out of control.

This is one of those tantalizing clues in the stories of Saul's sex life. It seems so very cliché, but like most men with money and power, he apparently had a trophy, a woman who could make him feel important, make him feel like an alpha among the boys because he was able to bed the best-looking babe.

Trophy hunters of all sorts have one thing in common: whether the trophies are people or animals, they want to have some visible evidence and validation of their prowess. In the interest of full public disclosure, you should know that I have a taxidermied buck head mounted in my basement, an eight-pointer I bagged with a nearly miraculous shot in a northern New York swamp. But I'm not a trophy hunter. I've got little interest in going to Africa and sitting over a pile of garbage so I can kill a lion and have it mounted on the wall of my man cave and then tell my buddies about what a great hunter I am.

I believe this desire for evidence and external validation is one of the many reasons pornography has nearly universal appeal. Pornography is the opportunity to vicariously enter a world where we imagine ourselves to be someone we are not, and someone we were never meant to be, either because we don't like who we are sexually, or we chafe at the God-given boundaries to our sexuality and trespass through the surreal images of porn. Aside from the fact that it is intoxicating and therefore addictive, porn seems to be especially appealing to those who believe their sexuality is their own private business.

I heard a preacher say that using the internet is like living next to a whorehouse with glass walls. At no other time in human history has there been the constant and instant opportunity for men and women to be transported to a place where they can see anyone or anything they've ever imagined. Eyes become entry points through which the very real toxins and poisons of immorality are injected into the bodies, souls, and relationships on this side of the screen.

The harmful effects of pornography on the life of the believer, the family, and the church are well documented. But its availability and power can also provide us with the opportunity to convert its evil energy into the fuel to propel us into the presence of God. Nearly every time we turn on our computer or TV, we'll have the opportunity to make a decision to acknowledge the rightful authority of God to govern our sexuality and His circumcision of our hearts.

Thoughts for Personal Reflection:

- We live in an age when personal sexual preferences and

identities have been elevated to such a high status that they regularly compete with the authority of the New Testament's guidelines for sexuality and marriage. What are your thoughts on this?

- Can our personal sexual insecurities that prompt us to trespass God's boundaries be traced back to our insecurities as believers? Perhaps there is no clearer, no more direct, easy-to-see causation than our inability to find sexual security.

SECTION IV:
The Insecure Parent

CHAPTER 13

The Insecure Parent

"For as long as the son of Jesse lives on the earth, neither you nor your kingdom will be established. Therefore now, send and bring him to me, for he must surely die." But Jonathan answered Saul his father and said to him, "Why should he be put to death? What has he done?" Then Saul hurled his spear at him to strike him down; so Jonathan knew that his father had decided to put David to death.
— 1 Samuel 20:31-33

Saul was a volcano. A ready-to-erupt-at-any-second patriarch glowering over the landscape of his family. I imagine smoke venting from the peak of his crowned head, and I can almost hear the rumble of seismic anger that sends everyone in the house running to the basement for cover or trying to appease him with conciliatory offerings that they lay at his feet like pagans bringing offerings of fruit and flowers to the altar of their volcano god idol.

But there's nothing anyone can do to stop his eruptions. Sons get spears thrown at them, daughters have marriages annulled, and his descendants pay for his sins with their own blood.

At the end of his life, all the curses and ills that were being superheated by the insecurities deep within the mantle of his soul erupted for the last time. It was then that a pyroclastic wave of molten disasters raced down his slopes and incinerated his sons and grandsons. His final eruption sent toxic ash spewing into the atmosphere, ash that rained down on his two daughters and buried them in lifetimes of heartache, loneliness, and grief.

Like archeologists unearthing the ancient city of Vesuvius, we find Saul's descendants entombed in the pages of Scripture, and the legacy of the house of Saul a mummified mausoleum and cautionary cairn, forever warning all of us about what happens to those who live closest to the dangerous slopes of the profoundly insecure. We discover them asphyxiated in the prime of life, frozen in the deadly fallout of their patriarch's sin.

If you're thinking that all this volcanic imagery is a bit too dramatic, I'd ask that you first consider the brief biographies of Saul's direct descendants before you pass judgment on these graphic lava and ash images, and afterward decide if being swept away by pyroclastic waves or being buried in toxic ash are fair comparisons for what happened to his children and grandchildren.

Chapter 14

Saul's Kids

Overcoming parental insecurity involves taking responsibility for our children's well-being

Now the sons of Saul were Jonathan and Ishvi and Malchi-shua; and the names of his two daughters were these: the name of the firstborn Merab and the name of the younger Michal.
— 1 Samuel 14:49

So the king took the two sons of Rizpah the daughter of Aiah, Armoni and Mephibosheth whom she had borne to Saul...
— 2 Samuel 21:8a

Saul was a father of no less than eight children. We know the most about his oldest son, Jonathan, and his youngest daughter, Michal. Because of Jonathan's friendship with David and Michal's marriage to him, we have more information in the Bible about their lives than about those of the other siblings. But even though we know far less about the other six, what we do know is not good. In fact, it's really, really bad.

Three of his sons, including Jonathan, die in combat alongside their father at the battle of Mount Gilboa. After that battle, the corpses of Saul and his sons are strung up on the city wall of Beth-shan and left to rot as a gruesome commemoration by the victorious Philistines. The Philistines also decapitate Saul and parade his severed head and his weapons throughout their land in a macabre traveling sideshow, heralding their victory over both the nation of Israel and the now headless and humiliated king with whom they had done battle for nearly two generations.

When news of the defiled bodies reaches the city of Jabesh-gilead, a squad of men travel by night to remove the bodies from public display. Later, they cremate the rotted remains as a final act of respect to Saul and his sons for rescuing their city so many years before.

After the death of his father and three brothers, a fourth son, Ish-bosheth (presumably absent from the battle of Mount Gilboa), is installed as a regional rival to King David. But his authority and power are not only illegitimate, they are also completely dependent upon Abner, his father's uncle and military commander. Ish-bosheth is Abner's puppet, a king in name only who serves as a figurehead for Abner's regional government in the land of Benjamin, where the people were still loyal to the memory of their tribesman. But the relationship between Ish-bosheth and Abner is short-lived.

Ish-bosheth just doesn't get it. He fails to understand that both his title and his authority exist only because of his uncle's schemes and the remnant of the army that is still loyal to Abner. When he discovers that Abner has been sleeping with Rizpah, his father's trophy concubine, he foolishly confronts him about this affront to his father's reputation. Abner gives birth to the proverbial cow, lashing back at Ish-bosheth with everything he has, reminding the boy of his place and vowing to transfer all of his political and military power to King David. He sends envoys to David to arrange for the surrender of the land's armies so that they would be consolidated under David's leadership.

Abandoned and afraid, Ish-bosheth sees his little fiefdom quickly crumble. He is forced to return his sister Michal to her husband David as part of the terms of surrender. Soon afterward, Abner is murdered by David's general Joab in revenge for the life of his brother Asabel, whom Abner killed years earlier during a skirmish between the two factions. Now completely defenseless, Ish-bosheth is assassinated and decapitated by two of his own lieutenants while taking his midday nap. Apparently, the tribe of Benjamin's crown-capped pates were quite detachable.

Saul's other two other sons, Armoni and Mephibosheth, who were born to his concubine Rizpah, were executed by the Gibeonites. These two sons, along with five of Saul's grandsons, who were born to his eldest daughter Merab, all died the same day. The death of these seven descendants of Saul is probably the most heinous of all the violent and unnecessary tragedies that befell his progeny.

The seven men were surrendered to the Gibeonites in an ill-advised attempt to atone for Saul's violation of the covenant that had been made with them by the nation of Israel when they first invaded the Promised Land. These men were taken from their homes, bound, and then marched to the gallows as human sacrifices meant to atone for the sins of their grandfather. After the execution, their corpses, like those of Saul and his sons, were left unburied and hung in public for five months in Saul's hometown as a superstitious totem of human flesh (2 Samuel 21:1-6).

As if the just God of Heaven could be appeased by the murder of someone's descendants. As if He would look down on the decaying bodies of innocent men and smile on the land. How silly. How sad. Rizpah kept vigil for her own sons' and their half-brothers' bodies for five sleepless months. By day and night she guarded the rotting flesh of those men from the birds and wild beasts who wanted to feast on the remains. By day she beat away the vultures who wanted to peck out their eyes, and by night she tended a fire that kept the predators and scavengers at bay.

The only male descendant of Saul who survives is his grandson Mephibosheth, the son of Jonathan (Saul had a son who shared the same name), who suffered a crippling accident as a child that left him lame in both feet for the rest of his life (2 Samuel 4:4). And though he survives, his legacy and story is anything but good. Shortly after David establishes his authority, he remembers his covenant with his friend Jonathan and makes inquiries to see if there are any surviving descendants of Jonathan to whom he can show kindness. Mephibosheth is quickly discovered, and David becomes his benefactor. The new king restores his family's lands and invites the disabled man to become a regular at his royal dinner table.

The only other thing we know about Mephibosheth is that his own servant Ziba indicts him in a failed coup against David several years later. David rewards Ziba with all of his master's lands. Later, when Mephibosheth is summoned to appear before David to give account of himself, he pleads his innocence. But it is unclear if David fully believes his story, because the king restores only one-half of the family lands that had been given to his servant. So it is likely that Saul's only surviving male descendant limps off the pages of Scripture as the man who betrayed his father's best friend.

So just to recap: All six of Saul's sons and five of his grandsons die violent deaths, and the sole surviving grandson looks to have gotten involved in an attempt to overthrow the government of his father's covenantal friend.

But wait, there's even more!

Let's not forget about Saul's daughters.

Merab

His oldest, Merab, the mother of the five sons who were executed for their grandfather's crimes, was left to live out her days with the unimaginable grief of losing not just one child, but five on the same day.

Many of us probably know something about the heartache of a child's death, either from our own loss or that of someone we are close to. For any parent who outlives a child, there is a grief so profound that many mental healthcare professionals believe it can only be compared to the loss of a loving spouse. We can only imagine what it would be like to lose five sons in one day. A grief that perhaps no mother could understand better than Alleta Sullivan.

Imagine: early on the morning of January 12, 1943, Alleta's husband Thomas had just gone out the front door of their Iowa home on his way to work, when three men in uniform approached him. A lieutenant commander, a doctor, and a chief petty officer were coming up the walkway and met him there.

The commander said:

"I have some news for you about your boys."

"Which one?" asked Thomas.

"I'm sorry," the officer replied.

"All five."

All five. I don't know how those two words could pass into the ear, enter the mind, and not kill the soul of a parent. I can hear Thomas asking, "Could you say that again please?" The commander says it again, the unimaginable words hanging in the air along with the man's frosty breath.

I can see him leading the officers into the kitchen, where they say the same words to Alleta, who is clutching a dishtowel. The words strike her, and for a few seconds she seems unaffected by the blow. Then her legs give out under the weight of those two simple words. The officers help the couple find their way onto the davenport in the parlor. I see them staring at the five pictures over the fireplace as they hear the details of how the USS *Juneau*, the ship which all of their sons were aboard, was sunk by the Japanese in the Pacific about two months before.

I can also see Merab. She is looking at nothing off on the horizon, while her sons are shackled and marched off to their senseless executions. I can see molten tears running down her face and the words *all five* vaporizing her hope. I hear her out in the fields at night, sleepless, alone, trying to pray. But all she can do is curse her father. Cursing him for his selfishness. Cursing him for his unbridled rage. Cursing him for his lust for revenge. Cursing his memory and forever fixing the responsibility for her five sons' deaths upon her father.

Finally, there's Saul's youngest daughter, Michal.

Michal

As the father of three daughters, I think the story of Saul's daughter Michal hits closest to home for me. I've never experienced the death of a child, and I don't have any sons. And even though I will never feel the cultural weight of a hyper-patriarchal culture, an age when daughters could be shuffled about like livestock and married off against their wills, perhaps I can feel the weight of Michal's burden the most.

Michal, the baby of the family, didn't escape her father's curse of insecurity either. Her big mistake was falling in love with David, the oh-so-handsome hero-heartthrob, best buddy of her brother, and archenemy of her dad. When her father gets wind of her infatuation, he gladly arranges for her to marry the young man she has been pining for. For a short season she must have thought her father was the sweetest daddy in the whole wide world. What other dad would use his political muscle to secure the affections of the man his little darling had fallen for?

But Saul didn't give a fig for his daughter's feelings. He only arranged the marriage to get David killed by asking for the dangerous dowry of one hundred Philistine foreskins. This meant exposing Michal's beau to another round of military clashes in which a single arrow or thrust of a sword would have eliminated Saul's problem. Of course, David had different plans. He successfully leads his men against the Philistines and doubles down on the dowry, laying two hundred Philistine foreskins at the kings's feet, and then stands with the king's daughter at the altar.

The leveraging of a daughter's romantic feelings, without a hint of remorse or consideration for her emotions or well-being, exposes the depravity of Saul's heart. Exploiting a child for one's personal agenda and ambitions is surely one of the most disgusting things any parent could ever become guilty of. And while David manages to avoid the blades and arrows of the Philistines, Michal is not so fortunate. His young wife unwittingly becomes the victim of her father's sordid plot to wed her to his enemy.

After Michal's wedding, her father's irrational hatred for David is fully unmasked. It is right around this time that the profoundly insecure king throws his spear at David for the first time, during one of those musical deliverance sessions David had been recruited to perform. David escapes, and Saul's spear is left dangling in the wall.

Later that same night, Saul sends assassins to David's house to lie in wait to murder him in an early morning ambush. Michal gets wind of the plot, and like any young and in-love wife, her loyalties now lie with her husband, and she helps David escape out the window of their home. In the morning, when Saul discovers that she has abetted the escape of her husband, he is furious, and she has to lie to her father and tell him that David threatened her with death if she did not help him escape.

It's easy to imagine David sitting on the edge of the window saying goodbye to his young bride. He gently wipes the tears from her cheek and gathers her into his arms; they kiss one last time, and then he slides down the rope and disappears into the night to begin his life as a fugitive. Michal would have had no idea that things would never be the same for her again. That her personal life was doomed because of her father's insecurities, and that the stormy sea that her marriage barque was plunged into that night was a tempest no couple could expect to weather.

Soon after David's escape, her father both annulled her marriage and married her off to another man named Palti. During those years of separation, David began to practice polygamy, and he fathered numerous children with other women. Because Davd was a fugitive, any attempt on Michal's part to communicate with him during his exile would have been seen as treason. So there are no love notes, no birthday cards, no texts, no FaceTime. Just years of silence ever widening the gulf between the newlyweds.

As we've already learned, David negotiated Michal's return to him as part of the treaty with Abner, but the years of silence and separation have taken their toll. David's other wives compete for his affections, and Michal bears the stigma of having been the wife of another man who is still living and pining for her return. It's safe to assume that their marriage was not just being buffeted by storms, but was at the bottom of the sea.

It's in this context that we read about the episode for which Michal is best known. We find her looking down from a window again. But this time, she's not saying goodbye to her lover, she is literally and figuratively looking down on David as he dances in the streets on the day the ark is returned to Jerusalem. When he comes back home that day, she chides him for leading the victory parade in his underwear during the festivities, and she includes a none-too-subtle dig about the "maids" whom she must have seen ogling her athletic and handsome husband as he was wiggling about in his skivvies.

David defends his exuberant style of worship with the iconic line that he will be "even more undignified than this" (2 Samuel 6:22). His retort has found its way into both modern worship songs and teaching about demonstrative worship, and rightfully so, because the approval of man is not a prerequisite for the authentic worship of God. This is how Michal's criticism of David has made her the whipping girl of preachers and worship promoters who see her as emblematic of anyone who finds demonstrative worship offensive.

But David's spiky quip includes more than a teaching about demonstrative worship; he adds the cutting reminder to his long-estranged wife that God chose him above her father and her relatives. David has many redeeming qualities, but in this situation he proves himself to be anything but a sympathetic and understanding husband. For a woman who would still have been grieving the recent deaths of her father and brothers, having her ignoble family history thrown in her face must have been the coup de grâce for her all-but-dead marriage.

I want to let Michal off the hook, cut her some slack, and give her some understanding nods across the millennia. In spite of her imperfect critique of her husband's worship style, she deserves a lot of mercy. Knowing her backstory – her father's schemes, her long separation from her husband, and her forced marriage to another man – should give us a lot more grace for this young woman who found herself in an impossible situation.

She wanders off the pages of Scripture with this epitaph: "And Michal the daughter of Saul had no child to the day of her death" (2 Samuel 6:23). A sad footnote about a lonely young woman with a polygamous husband and a poor excuse for a father.

So what kind of parent is it who would throw a spear at his child? What kind of parent is so obsessed with his own success, reputation, and position that he would be willing to have his son executed to ensure it? What kind of parent would leverage his daughter's affections to try to have his new son-in-law killed? What kind of parent would drag his children and grandchildren into the consequences of his own rebellion, and in doing so, condemn them to violent death and unimaginable grief?

A profoundly insecure parent like Saul, that's who.

If we ever lack motivation to address insecure behaviors, we can just take a look at our kids, grandkids, and spiritual offspring for inspiration. If there ever comes a time when we start to think that it's okay to put off substantial change for another day, we ought to take a long hard look at the impact our insecure behaviors will have on our progeny and start off on a new course immediately. We don't have a minute to spare.

Before we leave this look at Saul's children, we should also note that the parenting dynamic for ancient kings and leaders of any kind is different for a couple of reasons. First, the children of leaders live under a higher-powered magnifying glass than other kids do. The coach's son and the preacher's daughter often find themselves being held to different standards than other kids on the team or in the choir. It's a universal burden of life lived in community, which only becomes a big deal if the leader succumbs to the temptation to subject his or her children to those standards and expectations in order to accommodate detractors or placate critics.

Wise parents in leadership roles should be mindful of not allowing their children to carry the weight of inappropriate scrutiny and unrealistic expectations. When leaders see their kids weighed down by those things, they can easily relieve them of these burdens by saying things like, "We don't worry about what other people expect from you; we're only concerned with the things our God and our family worry about." They can and should also feel completely empowered to directly address the people who are the ongoing source of this kind of scrutiny if it becomes necessary to do so. Simply put, kids need to know that their parents have their backs.

A second reason the parenting dynamic for Christian leaders is different is Biblical. A New Testament qualification for an elder is that "he must be one who manages his own household well, keeping his children under control with all dignity ...but if a man does not know how to manage his own household, how will he take care of the church of God?" (1 Timothy 3:4). He must also be "above reproach, the husband of one wife, having children who believe, not accused of dissipation or rebellion" (Titus 1:6). These are sobering qualifications, because children are one of the few ways outsiders can know something about the inner workings of a leader's non-public life.

A problem child is never the Christian leader's problem that needs to be fixed so he or she can enter into or remain in a leadership role. Children are simply the imperfect reflections and gauges of the leader's family life. If all of a leader's kids are a mess, that should be a pretty good clue that something else is out of order. And the reverse is also true; if a leader's kids are well-adjusted and spiritually thriving, that's also a pretty good indicator that the man or woman of God behind the microphone is the same person behind the front door.

Thoughts for Personal Reflection:

- How does the story of Saul's family history make you feel?
- If we believe that children are a reflection of a parent's spirituality, how precisely should this principle be applied?
- At what point do you think the behavior of one's children could disqualify someone from a leadership role?

CHAPTER 15

Whoever It Takes

OVERCOMING PARENTAL INSECURITY INVOLVES PLACING MORE IMPORTANCE ON OUR CHILDREN THAN ON OUR CAREERS OR SUCCESSES

> *Now the men of Israel were hard-pressed on that day, for Saul had put the people under oath, saying, "Cursed be the man who eats food before evening, and until I have avenged myself on my enemies." So none of the people tasted food.... "For as the Lord lives, who delivers Israel, though it is in Jonathan my son, he shall surely die."*
> *— 1 Samuel 14:24, 39*

I like working with people who are willing to do whatever it takes to get a job done. People who show up for work even when they don't feel well, or who stay late when a deadline is looming. The whatever-it-takes, can-do attitude is attractive to me. It's also a common thread in the lives of just about every person who has ever been successful. Adversity is part and parcel of the human experience, and no one should expect to achieve much of anything without hard work, perseverance, determination, personal discipline, and grit.

I especially admire men and women who do whatever it takes to ensure that their children are well cared for. Moms who work two jobs or spend long nights with one eye open and both ears listening to hear if their sick child will wake up in the night. Dads who attend night classes to finish their education or keep working at jobs that that are sometimes both difficult and unfulfilling. Let's be clear: working hard does not a workaholic make. Hard work, perseverance, determination, personal discipline, and grit – these character traits are not the opposite of grace, but the by-product of it.

The Apostle Paul, the man who understood grace more clearly perhaps than anyone who has ever walked on the face of the earth, said, "But by the grace of God I am what I am, and His grace toward me did not prove vain; but I labored even more than all of them, yet not I, but the grace of God with me" (1 Corinthians 15:10). Yeah, Paul worked his proverbial tail off to fulfill his destiny and achieve the goals that God had set before him.

But hard work and personal achievement have their limitations, both in the spiritual and the natural.

Spiritually, it will never make us right with God. Work does not have the ability to tip the scales of eternity in our favor. In Christ alone, and in His completed work upon the cross, is salvation. Any recipe for salvation that requires even a pinch of human effort is false. Any religious system that has even a molecule of human achievement as a necessary ingredient is a deadly poison to mankind, and ultimately an insult to the complete work of Christ, and something that the Father will never taste.

In the natural, work also has limits. Unceasing labor ruins both mental and physical health. Thankfully, most modern nations now have laws that protect employees from the unregulated hours and hazardous working conditions that were the scourge of earlier generations. But for some people, the desire to be successful or to achieve notoriety and celebrity can become an obsession that drives them to dangerous places. An all-consuming passion that has the potential to destroy both their lives and their families.

It's not always easy to know exactly when righteous hard work turns into an unhealthy and destructive lifestyle. I don't have a map that shows exactly where that line is. But I do know that there is a line we all can be sure of, a clearly defined boundary that should never be crossed.

It's the line that is crossed when *whatever it takes* turns into *whomever it takes*.

The moment we start to sacrifice people to reach our goals, we've crossed the line. When, in spite of failing marriages, maladjusted children, and lost friendships, we continue to plow forward with our schedules and agendas, we've gone too far. More often than not, this unrestricted and unregulated desire for achievement and success is fueled by a profound level of insecurity.

Insecurity is a powerful propellant. If we could pump insecurity into the fuel tanks of rockets, we could visit the stars. We've already mentioned how successful and talented people often confess that their insecurities are in fact the high-octane motivator that drives them to outperform their peers, or make monumental sacrifices to rise to the top of their professions. But the hot-burning fuel of insecurity is not easy to regulate. It can set the soul afire and burn down our homes. Fueled by insecurity, the ungoverned engine of achievement can drive us so fast that anything and anyone that stands in our way is going to get run over. Even our children.

This is exactly what happened to both King Saul and the judge Jephthah. Both of these men were dynamic leaders to be sure, but they were also fathers. Both of these men were driven by such a profound sense of insecurity and became so obsessed with winning that they were willing to not just do whatever it took to win, but use whomever it took. For men like Saul and Jephthah, the old saying applies: "Winning isn't everything; it's the only thing."

In the Scripture portion that begins this section, we read about Saul invoking two foolish oaths. Actually, describing his oaths as foolish really doesn't do this passage any justice. If there was ever a place that it would seem appropriate to use expletives to describe someone's actions, this might must be the place. I'm not sure there are any polite words that could adequately capture just how %$^&!!&*# ridiculously evil, idiotic, and utterly insane both of these oaths were.

The first oath compels his soldiers to participate in an all-day fast while engaged in combat. Anyone with a military background or even a sliver of common sense would know that this has to be about the dumbest thing a military leader could ever do. There's probably no other experience humans can participate in that is more fatiguing than combat. You've probably heard something about MREs (meals ready to eat); these are the tan-colored, plastic-wrapped rations that US soldiers eat when they are in the field. You may also have seen them distributed during disaster relief efforts, when these meals are airlifted into remote locations where survivors or refugees are stranded.

According to the Army's own data and research, "Three MREs a day provide warfighters with a minimum of 3,600 calories, satisfying their nutritional needs for most missions." However, Julie Smith of the Combat Feeding Directorate points out that "there are some instances during exceptionally heavy activity where warfighters will need between 4,500 and 6,000 calories per day."[1]

We can only guess how many calories sword-wielding Bronze Age infantry soldiers would have needed to keep their strength up. But Saul was so obsessed with winning that he bound his army with an oath not to eat a single thing, because of a superstitious belief that God would be more likely to help the Israelites if they engaged in some ascetic religious exercise while chasing down their enemies.

The second foolish oath is made by Saul the next day, when he becomes convinced that God has withheld His blessing on their mili-

---

[1] Zanchi, Joseph, and Alexandra Foran. "'More' Is Better." U.S. Army, 10 Mar. 2014, www.army.mil/article/121545/more_is_better. Accessed 24 Jun. 2018.

tary advance because of some hidden sin within the camp. He swears an oath that the offending person, even if it is his own son, will be executed. Lots are cast, and Jonathan is discovered to have been the man who unknowingly broke his father's oath by eating some wild honey he discovered in the forest the previous day. Oops.

Thankfully, Saul does not follow through on his oath to execute his son; Jonathan is rescued by the people, who intercede for him and assuage the wrath of Saul by reminding him that it was Jonathan himself who was the hero of the day. And while we can be grateful for the last-minute stay of execution, we'll never know how badly this father-son relationship was damaged by this foolish oath, except to note that Saul must have done irreparable harm when he looked his son in the eye and said, "You shall surely die, Jonathan" (1 Samuel 14:44).

I wish this was the only story in the Bible about a father who is so obsessed with winning that he is willing to have his own children killed to secure a victory. But there is another, similar story with an even more tragic ending.

The Saddest Story in the Bible

> *Jephthah made a vow to the Lord and said, "If You will indeed give the sons of Ammon into my hand, then it shall be that whatever comes out of the doors of my house to meet me when I return in peace from the sons of Ammon, it shall be the Lord's, and I will offer it up as a burnt offering."*
> *— Judges 11:30-31*

Leaders with shame and insecurity issues seem especially prone to making inappropriate sacrifices in the pursuit of victory. We've already seen in detail that Saul's sense of shame was rooted in his city's and tribe's immoral history, and that it was a driving factor in his insecurities. The power of shame-driven insecurity is on full display in the life of another leader in Israel's history: the judge Jephthah.

You might not be familiar with Jephthah; he doesn't have the kind of biography that Sunday school teachers or preachers are going to share too often. But as we will soon see, he offered up his daughter in a misguided attempt to fulfill the conditions of a vow similar to Saul's, which he invoked to secure a military victory. Feel free to read his entire story in the book of Judges at a later time, but for now I'll give you the condensed version of his life and the tragedy he is best known for.

Jephthah's mother was a prostitute. When his younger half-brothers (born to his father's wife) came of age, they kicked Jephthah out of the house and wrote him out of the will. Then he was exiled from the community by the city elders and became some kind of outlaw-warlord in the land of Tob. Tob was the rugged borderland between Israel and Ammon in what is today northwestern Jordan. It is from this isolated location that he gathers to himself a gang of unsavory types. During this time the Ammonites begin to conduct raids on his former community.

Desperate for protection, the elders of Gilead swallow their pride and turn to the only valiant warrior their city has ever produced. They come to him with their hats in their hands and make him an offer: "Defeat our enemies, and we will make you our chief." This is truly an offer he can't refuse. A victory over the Ammonites would not only vindicate him and his mom, but also allow him to exact a bit of revenge on his half-brothers, who booted him from the house and inheritance. This is why he makes such a rash vow to sacrifice the first thing that comes out of his house when he returns to his home.

Initially, he tries to negotiate a peace with the Ammonites, but when negotiations break down, he goes to war. A war he quickly wins. When he returns home, elated and ready to celebrate his victory and rise to power and prestige with his family, the first thing he sees as he comes to the family home is his beloved only child coming out of the house. His joy turns into mourning, and he only manages to grant her a two-month reprieve. But after those two months, the Scriptures tell us that he "did to her according to the vow." Well-meaning Bible teachers always seem to be trying to clean up this horrible story, explaining that Jephthah didn't actually follow through on his vow to have his own daughter killed. I hope these teachers are right, but the clearest, simplest reading of the passage doesn't give us much reason to believe that this filicide didn't happen. It's yet another example of the unredacted and unedited nature of Scripture that comes to us with all of its cultural bias, ancient ignorance, and gratuitous violence. But the lesson is clear. If we as parents ever begin to value our success to the degree that we are willing to sacrifice the health and well-being of our children, we have crossed a line that we were never meant to step over.

Before we exit this scene, we should pause a moment to doff our proverbial hats and have a moment of silence to remember that this family's history is both sacred and sad. If we were to go back in time to attend his daughter's funeral and stand around that freshly-covered grave with them, there wouldn't be a dry eye in the congregation. The violence, superstitions, and Biblical ignorance of that age are all jumbled together in a narrative about the son of a prostitute who became an outlaw, and then was willing to sacrifice his only child in exchange for a place of honor and respect in the community that had shamed him.

Thoughts for Personal Reflection:

- Both Saul and Jephthah are driven to succeed by a deep sense of family shame. Can you expand on whether or how this dynamic affects you?
- What are other sources of this kind of unhealthy obsession with winning?

Chapter 16

Cultural Insecurity

Overcoming parental insecurity involves abandoning unhealthy cultural norms

Now the sons of Eli were worthless men; they did not know the Lord...
— 1 Samuel 2:12

His sons, however, did not walk in his ways, but turned aside after dishonest gain and took bribes and perverted justice. Then all the elders of Israel gathered together and came to Samuel at Ramah; and they said to him, "Behold, you have grown old, and your sons do not walk in your ways. Now appoint a king for us to judge us like all the nations."
— 1 Samuel 8:3-5

I know a guy who lives in central Asia, and when he takes his kids to the park to play, people stare at him or talk about him when they think he's not looking. But the reason they do this isn't because they don't like him, or because his kids look different. It's because they live in a place where there are so few dads who spend time with their children that just the sight of a father pushing his kids on the swings or helping them down the slides creates a kind of buzz in the neighborhood.

Because he lives in a place where such a high percentage of children are fathered by men who want little or nothing to do with raising and nurturing them, his parenting methods have also gotten some of his neighbors questioning their own parenting norms and the practices of the generations that came before them. It's a place where the cultural norm of absentee fathers is so pervasive that virtually every family has been negatively impacted by it.

Unfortunately, absentee fathers are just one example of how unhealthy cultural norms create insecurities about how parents raise their kids. There are no less than five other culture-wide insecurities that have a profoundly negative impact on entire generations and regions, and all but one of these insecurities are on full display in the generations before and after Saul was a father.

No Successful Examples

Some cultures and communities don't have nearly enough successful families to model parenting to the next generation.

This is how it was for Saul when he became a dad. Neither Eli nor Samuel, the two spiritual leaders of the nation in the generations before Saul, seemed to know very much about how to raise kids. If they were alive today, it's unlikely that either of these men would be asked to speak at a parenting conference or would sell many how-to books on parenting. And even though Eli and Samuel were very different men spiritually and personally, their sons ended up in similar situations.

Eli was Samuel's mentor and the priest who presided over Israel during a time with little or no spiritual vibrancy. His tenure culminated with the highjacking of the Ark of the Covenant by the Philistines. On the same day that the ark was carried off, both of Eli's corrupted sons, Hophni and Phinehas, were killed in the battle. During the battle Eli sat by the side of the road, anxiously awaiting news from the front. When a disheveled messenger ran back to town and told him of his sons' deaths and the capture of the ark, he became a prophetic Humpty Dumpty and fell backward off his seat and broke his neck because he was so heavy. His enormous girth was irrefutable evidence that he participated in the sin of his sons by gorging himself on the meat that they extorted from worshipers bringing animal sacrifices to the temple.

Samuel, on the other hand, is a model of Biblical spirituality. He regularly heard from God and wasn't dragged into the graft and debauchery that Eli's sons were fond of. He wasn't beset by the spiritual lethargy and moral compromise of his mentor Eli, and he judged Israel for forty years without a hint of scandal. But like Eli, he seems to have lacked the ability to impart integrity to his own sons. And while the poor character of Hophni and Phinehas seems almost predictable in light of their father's carnal lifestyle, the fact that Samuel's sons turn out to be similar scoundrels comes as a bit of a surprise.

We discover this generational disconnect in Samuel's family when he was nearing retirement and appointed his two sons, Joel and Abijah, to serve as judges in his place. Unfortunately, they didn't possess the integrity of their father, and the Scriptures tell us they "turned aside after dishonest gain and took bribes and perverted justice" (1 Samuel 8:3). Because of their lack of integrity and Samuel's inability or unwillingness to remove them from their judgeships, the elders of Israel confronted Samuel and demanded that a king rule over them like the other nations around them. Samuel took this rejection of his sons personally, but God consoled him by telling him that the Israelites' demand for a king was actually a rejection of God as their King.

I guess we'll never know, but we can only wonder how different the history of Israel might have been if Samuel's sons had been able to imbibe the integrity of their father. Perhaps a certain tall farmer from Benjamin could have anonymously lived out his days hoeing weeds and chasing lost donkeys as Samuel's sons continued their father's legacy of righteously judging the nation.

The personal histories of these two families illustrate just how hard it is to parent when you don't have good examples nearby to learn from. And oftentimes, even personal spirituality like Samuel's isn't enough to impart our faith and values to our kids when everyone else around us seems to be completely inept at parenting. It's especially discouraging and confusing when young parents discover that the community and spiritual leaders who should be modeling some level of success in parenting have some really screwed-up kids. We can all feel some empathy for Saul and Ahinoam as they limped through their child-raising years on the heels of Eli's and Samuel's parenting examples. This inability to consistently impart values to children was a cultural issue that affected nearly all of ancient Israel's culture. Even David, a paragon of personal spiritual vitality in the subsequent generation, went on to face more than his share of challenges with his own children. His ability to impart his heart for God to his scions was inconsistent at best. It's as if that entire era of parents lived in a fog.

Before we continue on the subject of parental insecurity that springs from culture-wide issues, I want to give a big shout-out of thanks to the Gmitters, Websters, Coles, and other families like them for both modeling and mentoring my wife and me in parenthood. And for doing so in such a way that she and I were able to emulate their families' successes, so that by their examples and the grace of God, all three of our kids are thriving adults who are spiritually grounded. I know not everyone has the blessing of role models like we had, and we're keenly aware personally of just how powerful the presence of successful families can be in the reproduction of spiritually thriving children.

No Code Will Work

No codification or rigid formula of child-rearing will produce godly children.

Less-than-perfect parenting examples in the Bible didn't start with Eli and didn't stop with Saul. Remember that Adam and Eve managed to raise a killer without the help of first-person shooter video games, atheist college professors, or internet porn. Job had to sweep up the spiritual mess left behind by his hard-partying kids, nine out of twelve of Jacob's boys were slave traders, and David raised both a murderer and a rapist. The list goes on. But the reason it's so hard to find parental role models among Old Testament heroes of the faith is that raising God-loving kids is all about grace, not law. And this truth applies even to well-meaning parents today who make the mistake of codifying Christian parenting.

All parents wish there were some kind of parent-proof child-raising system that would guarantee that our *wunderkinder* will slide off the hot griddle of adolescence as mature adults every time. It's tempting to believe that educating our sons behind the thick walls of our homes or private schools means that they will never get arrested. Or to believe that putting purity rings on our daughters' fingers will be a more effective form of birth control than the pill. But there's no such guarantee, no formula, and no law that will ever take grace, and even some good old-fashioned mercy, out of the child-raising equation.

I'm sorry if the passion of my language and grittiness of my examples have struck an uncomfortable nerve with those of you who have experienced the heartache of having kids who got into real trouble. I'm not trying to condemn or judge, and I'm certainly not trying to sell you on yet another detailed and comprehensive parenting strategy that promises to give you perfect kids every time. What I'm trying to do is to prevent another generation from putting their faith and trust in a method of education or parenting more than in the person of Christ.

I feel terrible for the families who have bought into a method but forgot about the Man. They then have to suffer through the disillusionment and pain of watching their kids fall into some pretty deep crevasses when they had all kinds of misplaced confidence that those things would never happen to them. Meanwhile, the authors and so-called experts go off and revise their theories and edit their books so they can experiment on another generation.

I'm equally passionate about how awesome children become when a godly parenting culture joins forces with practical and grace-infused teaching that is then applied by prayerful and humble parents. My experience and observation has been that godly children become the rule, not the exception, in these kinds of families. These parents understand that no religious system rooted in law is going to consistently produce children with authentic Christian beliefs. Personally, I don't want my kids to just mimic or ape my religion, or even embrace my theological distinctives if they thoughtfully and prayerfully reach different convictions than I have. All I want for them is to know Jesus and experience His transformative grace.

Nuclear Insecurity

It's hard to be confident about embracing the nuclear family model in cultures that have rejected or forsaken it.

I'm not sure how it is for those of you who grew up in other places, but it's easy for most of us who grew up in America to assume that the parents of previous generations knew what they were doing when it came to raising their kids. Most Americans can look back on the good old days and believe that the children we see in those sepia-toned pictures never interrupted adults when speaking, ate all their vegetables without fussing, did their homework by candlelight, and went to bed as happy as John-Boy.

I think some of this nostalgia is actually warranted, not because the good old days were always good – and we know that they were anything but perfect – but because many of our not-too-distant ancestors lived in a time when the cultural norms of the day demonstrated a healthy way to raise kids. Only now, as Western culture has continued to detach itself from the norm of having a mom and a dad raising their kids under the same roof, do we see the wholesale negative consequences of having more than half of our children in the vacuum of non-nuclear families.

In 2014 the government reported that only 46% of American children were being raised in what we now refer to as a traditional nuclear family. This is not an indictment against folks who find themselves raising their kids alone, or grandparents raising their grandkids. But the facts are that children raised in non-traditional models of family are at about twice the risk for nearly every negative outcome, and no amount of hoping or pretending will change these statistics.

In spite of the statistical evidence, large segments of our culture bristle at even the suggestion that the nuclear family is the ideal place to raise children. Pundits and critics are fond of highlighting and magnifying the excesses and ignorance that sometimes characterized traditional families of the past as a way of obfuscating and deflecting the conversation. But for all the criticism and fault-finding, the fact remains that children raised in a home where both parents live together are half as likely to be raised in poverty, engage in risky behaviors, or end up in any kind of institution later in life.

By the time Saul became a dad, Israel was a nation not too dissimilar to ours today; it too had become unhinged. And like all unsecured doors, it lost the ability to keep out the things it was supposed to keep out, and keep in the things it was supposed to keep in. This is why Saul and Ahinoam found themselves flapping in the parenting wind near the end of that era when the Bible's own historical indictment of that age says, "In those days there was no king in Israel; everyone did what was right in his own eyes" (Judges 21:25).

Information Insecurity

Parents are both insecure and confused about child-raising because of the massive amount of information on parenting.

This was one parenting challenge that Saul and Ahinoam didn't face. We've already touched on the information phenomenon in our conversation about romantic relationships – that more options don't necessarily lead to better choices when it comes to dealing with things like insecurity. This is why parenting can feel an awful lot like trying to drive a car full of hungry people who are all yelling directions to the restaurant to you at the same time. Except the voices from the backseat are yelling about the destinies of our kids, and not the virtues of chicken over beef.

My guess is that about 90% of the advice dispensed by books, blogs, and speakers is actually pretty good. But other than the 10% of poisonous foolishness, the biggest problem with having so much information is that we rarely, if ever, actually know the authors or bloggers personally. We don't get to watch their kids on the playground to see if all their parental wisdom actually works. Yet well-meaning parents, all hungry for answers and willing to do almost anything to raise successful children, will sometimes embrace drive-through parenting principles and methods based solely on the anecdotes of dynamic presenters or the cheery pictures of perfect-looking families posted on a homepage.

Many of us were raised in homes with a pretty high level of dysfunction, and so we're desperate not to repeat the mistakes of our parents. Others have the misfortune of actually knowing the children of some of their community and spiritual leaders, and have perfectly logical and good reasons for not wanting to follow their advice or their examples. Not knowing where, or whom, to turn to, parents begin the search for strategies and tips from strangers. They read books and articles, attend seminars and conventions, and search out parenting advice and wisdom from every corner of the globe. It's overwhelming for almost everyone, and so informational overload and insecurity springs up because we are convinced that we can't possibly know how best to parent our own children.

It's a systemic, culture-wide issue that offers few specifics to parents who are trying to make sense out of the constant stream of reputedly expert advice that flows out of every form of media. With so much information pinballing around in our minds, it should be no surprise that many parents feel totally overwhelmed. There are dozens, if not hundreds of parenting philosophies and schools of thought to choose from, many of which seem to be polar opposites of one another.

After a while, most parents eventually give up on the dream of finding the perfect system of child-raising and just muddle through those years with their hybridized and piecemeal handbook – a cut-and-paste mishmash of opinions, convictions, and techniques that we apply with varying levels of consistency and success on our kids. And you know what? That's a good thing, because parenting is an imperfect art, and in the middle of all the noise and chaos of raising children is the grace of God.

Authority Insecurity

Our culture is overpopulated by parents who are insecure about exercising their rightful authority over their kids.

Two examples of this authority insecurity are parents whose goal is to be best friends with their child and drone parents. The latter used to be called helicopter parents, but they've been upgraded to drone parents because they hover above their kids, ready to fire their laser-guided letters, legal suits, and sideline rants at any teacher, administrator, or coach who gets in the way of their little terrorist.

All parents have blind spots when it comes to their children. I know I do. Child-sized cataracts that cloud our vision enough to go the extra thousand miles with our kids when everyone else has long ago packed it in. But "blind spots," or what might be more accurately called "soft spots," become potentially disastrous when it comes to correcting and punishing them.

We've already noted that Eli's two sons, Hophni and Phinehas, were given over to debauchery and graft. They were, in the words of Scripture, "worthless men; they did not know the Lord" (1 Samuel 2:12). Today they would just be known as dirtbags. They were priests who got involved in extorting portions of the sacrifices from worshipers and in having sex with the women who worked at the temple. And while Eli didn't personally get involved in all of their sins, his bulk revealed enough of his guilt that he failed to properly investigate the way his sons got all those fatty cuts of sacrificial barbecue he was stuffing his piehole with.

Eventually, the reports about his sons' sins started to become public, and he was finally compelled to say something to them. Unfortunately, he was more interested in his family's reputation than his family's holiness. He didn't actually rebuke them for their crimes, but rather just underscored that the rumors about them were not good and asked them why they did those things. I've seen some curious things about this section of Scripture that I think will shed some light on some of the present-day confusion about parental authority.

I have a Bible that uses bold-faced headings for each section, and the passage where Eli asks his sons about their behavior is actually under a heading that reads, "Eli Rebukes His Sons." The next chapter is the famous account of God speaking to Samuel when he was a boy sleeping near the ark, the passage that is a favorite of Sunday school coloring pages and preschool flannel board lessons. But the word from God that little Samuel got was anything but child friendly, because it was about the pending and lethal judgment of God on Eli and his entire family. And the reason clearly given for this judgment is that Eli did not rebuke his sons.

I'm not sure how this kind of gaffe slips by the translators and editors, but I do know that if God said Eli didn't rebuke his sons, then he didn't rebuke his sons. I think a partial explanation for this editorial blunder is that our culture has come to understand the word *rebuke* differently than God does. Like Eli's, today's parental fascination with wanting to know why our kids do bad things has replaced our responsibility to rebuke them when the situation calls for it. Somehow our parental myopia wants to believe that if our little cherubs sin, there must be an explanation other than the fact that they are prone to sin along with the rest of humanity.

One commentator even goes as far as to cite this passage as an example of Scripture contradicting itself. The commentator noted that Eli did indeed rebuke his sons when he asked them, "Why do you do such things, the evil things I hear from all these people? No, my sons; the report is not good which I hear the Lord's people circulating" (1 Samuel 2:23-24). I wanted to yell at the commentator that this was not a rebuke; it was just a question followed up by some gossip.

And on the off chance you're still thinking that your vision of your kids is 20/20 and that you're too spiritual to have these kinds of blind spots, remember that even Samuel, who saw first-hand the consequences of having undisciplined sons in positions of authority, suffered from the same kind of blindness when he appointed his own sons as judges in his place. It took the elders of Israel to point this out to him, and even then he seems to have continued in his near-sighted belief that his boys were men of integrity, because he drags their names back into the narrative in his farewell address to the nation (1 Samuel 12:2).

Parenting is complicated and challenging enough in the best of times, so let's not make our job as parents even harder by thinking that we also need to become our children's psychoanalysts and discover why they sin. When your toddler grabs a toy from a playmate, don't ask her why; she took it because she has the same fascination with grabbing things that don't belong to her as her ancestor Eve had. And if you wake up late one night and discover your son in the basement having sex with his girlfriend, please don't ask him why!

I think a solution to this might be to have all hospitals and birthing centers start handing out brass stars to all the new moms and dads. But they should replace the word SHERIFF with the word PARENT. This way they'll be reminded that they have God's authority to be their child's authority. Because we live in such a litigious age, they'll probably have to include a disclaimer concerning psychopaths or sociopaths, but there's no one on the face of the earth more qualified to raise your kids than you!

Father Insecurity

The absence of responsible resident fathers creates emotional and social insecurity.

Before we leave this section, it would be good to go back to that playground in Asia and talk a little more about fathers. It's easy to imagine dads everywhere pushing their kids on swings, catching them when they skid down slides, or spotting them as they struggle across the monkey bars. But there's one piece of playground equipment it's really difficult for dads to play on with their kids, and that's the teeter-totter. Most dads have bellies that are way too big for that game!

Yet if we might be metaphorical for a moment, the see-sawing between fathers and their children is almost as old as Eden. Adam and Cain were literally the first long-distance father-son relationship. Since the dawn of time, fatherhood has been the stuff of fables, novels, movies, and teary campfire confessions. But this distance is a place of opportunity, especially for those who have some knowledge of God the Father. We have the opportunity to become moms and dads to a generation that has limped along with far too little parenting, and especially in the way of fathering.

Fathers are important because God is a Father. It's not as if the Almighty just fished around the heavens for the best metaphor with which to reveal Himself to humanity and then, after some conversations with His creative team, decided to go with the father idea. He is our Father in the same way that He is Love. Unlike us, He does not need to learn or grow into a character trait or role. He is who He is.

The issue of non-resident fathers is the greatest single social issue of our day, and the statistical evidence for this claim is overwhelming. Here in the United States, children raised in fatherless homes are more likely than their peers to suffer from a range of emotional, physical, and psychological problems. Heartbreakingly, they account for 71% of high school drop-outs, 85% of youth in prison, and 90% of runaways. They are 40% more likely to be sexually abused, and they experience higher rates of teen pregnancy, anxiety, depression, and suicide. The negative consequences can follow them throughout their lives; as adults, they're more likely to be unemployed or on financial assistance, to go through divorce, and to have children outside of stable relationships.[1] Compounding the

[1] Kruk, Edward. "Father Absence, Father Deficit, Father Hunger: The Vital Importance of Paternal Presence in Children's Lives." *Psychology Today*, 23 May 2012,

problem is the prevalence of resident fathers who are not present in the lives of their children.

Suffice it to say, this crisis in fatherhood is at the very core of the undermining and eroding of the Biblical template for family, which is the pattern for family life that gives children the best opportunity for a physically healthy, financially secure, and emotionally stable future. And as we have already seen, this is a worldwide issue. The legitimate, intense, and God-given desire to be in relationship with both a mother and a father is a compelling and irresistible force in the lives of hundreds of millions of young men and women who are living in fatherless homes all across the planet.

When responsible resident fathers are not part of a family, the vacuum created by their absence produces social and economic chaos that no society can indefinitely withstand because a growing percentage of our population finds itself at a higher risk for becoming non-contributing members of that society. Fatherlessness is swelling our prison population and overwhelming our mental health and social services providers as children suffer the consequences of this absenteeism. The innate, intense, and universal desire for male approval is a compelling negative force in the lives of hundreds of millions of young men and women who are living in fatherless homes all across the globe, and who are often searching for that approbation from the wrong things and the wrong people.

There is even a glimpse of this father vacuum in the lives of both Jonathan and David when they enter their covenantal friendship. I suspect the intensity of the friendship was driven in part by the lack of the fatherly approval their souls craved. They both wanted someone in their lives they could depend on no matter what happened to them, and they bestowed upon each other all the things that their dads didn't.

Remember, it was David who was left with the sheep when Samuel asked Jesse to bring all of his sons to the feast. I doubt any son, including David, would ever get over being forgotten by his father on a day like that. He was the Cinderella shepherd who was left out of the feasts and fights, stuck back on the farm to mop up after the sheep. After Jonathan died, it was David who lamented and sang of Jonathan, "Your love to me was more wonderful than the love of women" (2 Samuel 1:26). I suspect Jonathan was fulfilling the need for unconditional male approval that his brothers and dad never gave him.

---

https://www.psychologytoday.com/us/blog/co-parenting-after-divorce/201205/father-absence-father-deficit-father-hunger. Accessed 12 Dec. 2018.

And if Jonathan had been born in our generation, he would have worn a hole in his therapist's couch. If there was ever a man who had a right to have the proverbial daddy issues, it was him. I wonder how his counselor might have comported herself while Jonathan shared his story.

Therapist: Tell me about your father?

Jonathan: Well he's like the king, ya know, he's really tall and handsome.

Therapist: Yes, I've seen him on TV, what I meant was... tell me how you relate to him.

Jonathan: Umm, not too bad I guess... He did try to kill me a couple of times.

Therapist: Oh, ah... err... really... (as she digs her nails into the edge of the chair)

Jonathan: Yeah, and not just me; he also tried to kill my best friend a couple of times. See, he has this spear, and just after he forced my sister to marry this creeper dude, he throws it at...

While Jonathan finishes his story she is not really listening. She is dialing 911.

Thoughts for Personal Reflection:

- It's been said that a healed relationship with one's father is the most important qualification for Christian ministry. Do you agree?
- What are some examples of the codifying of child-raising?
- Why are some folks so intent on criticizing the nuclear family?

SECTION V:
The Insecure Leader

Chapter 17

The Insecure Leader

The young man who told him said, "By chance I happened to be on Mount Gilboa, and behold, Saul was leaning on his spear. And behold, the chariots and the horsemen pursued him closely. When he looked behind him, he saw me and called to me. And I said, 'Here I am.' He said to me, 'Who are you?' And I answered him, 'I am an Amalekite.' Then he said to me, 'Please stand beside me and kill me, for agony has seized me because my life still lingers in me.' So I stood beside him and killed him, because I knew that he could not live after he had fallen."
— 2 Samuel 1:6-10a

Saul's story ends with him leaning on his spear. The Philistines have overrun his army and killed his sons, and he is mortally wounded by their archers. He knows that if he is found alive, the enemy will mercilessly torture him to death, and so he asks his armor bearer to finish him off. But the loyal servant is unable to execute his master, and Saul has no choice but to fall on his own sword. But his harakiri-style suicide fails, and this is when a young scavenger finds the tall, handsome king crumpled up against his spear, helplessly waiting for the enemy to come and make his death as painful and ugly as they can.

Cutting rings off fingers and stealing coins from the dead on a battleground where the blood was still dripping and the victors had not taken their booty was not for the faint of heart nor the slow of foot. The Amalekite kid who found Saul must have been as quick as a fox, lurking around the edges of the battlefield and darting out to pinch anything from the dead and dying that could be quickly carried off. His sneakers were his best defense, so it's doubtful he would have been carrying anything as cumbersome as an iron sword. It's possible he was rifling through the pockets of Saul's already-dead armor bearer when the dying king heard him rummaging around and asked him to finish him off.

Saul's hopeless condition moves the young man to pity. He takes hold of the only weapon at hand: Saul's spear. When he pulls the spear from the ground, Saul slumps to the side, and the young man raises his arms and thrusts it through the gaps in the monarch's fancy armor in a merciful coup de grâce. That young treasure-hunting Amalekite must think he has hit the jackpot as he scurries back into the woods with the king's crown and bracelet. But it's difficult to fence the crown jewels, and he makes the fatal mistake of bringing his loot to David in hopes of a big payout. When he confesses that he was the one who finished Saul off, David rewards him by having him executed.

So as we come to the end of Saul's life, there can be zero doubt that his story is far more cautionary tale than inspirational biography. Sadly, the most redemptive thing about his story is that we now have a fairly complete list of the things profoundly insecure leaders often do and say. His life provides us with a checklist of symptoms that aren't too different from the kinds of lists we find on the internet that help us figure out whether we have a cold or the flu.

In this sense, Saul's life can become to us something like the lens of a microscope under which we can examine our own feelings and behaviors while they are still so small and benign that they might otherwise escape our notice. His story, as told through the Scriptures, has the ability to magnify our own insecurities long before they manifest as the life-ruining and legacy-stealing behaviors that plagued Saul during most of his forty-year reign.

Maybe profound insecurity could have been called Saulitis, or as Floyd McClung called it in his excellent book *The Father Heart of God*, "The Saul Syndrome."[1] But regardless of what we call it – sickness, syndrome, curse, it doesn't really matter – we just need to get over it. How I wish Saul would have asked a wise counselor to make a house call at the palace, a spiritual doctor of sorts who could have slipped in the back door and examined the sick king in private. He could have gently palpated Saul's soul with thoughtful questions, listened to his heart with a spiritual ear against his chest, and sent a biopsy of his insecurities off to the laboratory for closer examination. Afterward, the two could have sat and talked confidentially over a cup of tea about what was really ailing the tormented king.

But we don't have any record of him asking for that kind of help. He just stumbled from one disaster and bad decision to the next, while his insecurities grew ever larger and more malignant. And as we have already seen, they inflicted irreparable damage on himself, his family, and his nation. The good news for us is that we don't

---

[1] McClung, Floyd. *The Father Heart of God*. Harvest House, 2004.

have to be like Saul. We can ask for help. The last act in Saul's tragedy should galvanize our own resolve to walk away from the many temptations that insecurity can spawn.

In this final section we will explore fourteen destructive behaviors that Saul's profound insecurities inspired him to participate in. Fourteen ways he failed himself, his followers, and the nation he was called to lead. I'm trusting that this list of behaviors – these symptoms and manifestations – will help us not just to discover evidences of destructive insecurity, but also to convince and compel us to seek healing for even the very earliest indications of the disease of insecurity we might uncover in ourselves. These observations are simply an opportunity for self-diagnosis and the chance to separate even the smallest flecks of insecurity from ourselves long before they grow into the kind of profound insecurity that is so easy to see in Saul's leadership.

But before we move into the list, we need to talk about a few things.

First, if you're currently working for or serving under a profoundly insecure leader, you may have some difficult decisions to make in the not-too-distant future. You may have to walk away from him, resign, quit, or find a new position. Or you may feel compelled to address the issue with her privately or with a small group of colleagues in a kind of loving intervention. Or maybe you'll have to be like David and continue to muddle along, to learn to live under or hide from him until he gets fired, quits, or falls on his own sword.

But regardless of the course of action you feel inspired to take or how things turn out, there is one thing I'm begging you not to do. In fact, I just got on my knees and put my laptop up on my bed to beg you not to use these observations of Saul's insecurity as a way to indict the leader you're currently serving. David understood better than any other person just how dysfunctional and demonized Saul was, and yet he refused to attack Saul in any way. He didn't badmouth him, he didn't stage a coup d'état, and he didn't assassinate him in spite of two perfect opportunities to do so.

Also, when you discover some manifestation of insecurity in your own life, don't use it as an indictment of yourself. In the same way we don't have permission to attack the insecure leaders we serve under, we don't have permission to attack, condemn, or assassinate ourselves. Just because we discover a manifestation of insecurity in our lives and leadership does not mean that God wants to entomb us like nuclear waste that needs to be buried a mile underground in a salt mine in the desert. Remember, all of us have some insecurity in us; He unearths these things in us so we can turn away from them and become the secure leaders He has called us to be.

For the sake of convenience, I've grouped Saul's fourteen insecure behaviors into three categories: how insecure leaders hurt themselves, how they hurt their followers, and how they hurt their institutions. There's plenty of room for discussion about these imperfect groupings, because these behaviors have no precise boundaries, and they inevitably influence and carry over into different spheres of life, but my hope is that by divvying them up, even in this imperfect way, we'll be able to more quickly see the smallest traces of toxic insecurity long before it becomes something that ruins our lives and destroys our legacies.

We've already seen that insecurities have the ability to take all of us places we never intended to go. For Saul, one of those places was near a tamarisk tree, holding his spear while bribing and bullying his lieutenants to be more zealous in his misguided pursuit of David. Under the shade of that conifer is as good a place as any to start looking at the things insecure leaders say and do.

Chapter 18

Yes-Men Only

Secure leaders surround themselves with people who will tell them no

> *Then Saul heard that David and the men who were with him had been discovered. Now Saul was sitting in Gibeah, under the tamarisk tree on the height with his spear in his hand, and all his servants were standing around him. Saul said to his servants who stood around him, "Hear now, O Benjamites! Will the son of Jesse also give to all of you fields and vineyards? Will he make you all commanders of thousands and commanders of hundreds? For all of you have conspired against me so that there is no one who discloses to me when my son makes a covenant with the son of Jesse, and there is none of you who is sorry for me or discloses to me that my son has stirred up my servant against me to lie in ambush, as it is this day."*
> *— 1 Samuel 22:6-8*

Insecure leaders tend to surround themselves with family and friends who they believe will follow them without question and tell them only what they want to hear. They surround themselves with those who will blindly support them regardless of the situation, and they demand unwavering loyalty even when the facts contradict both their beliefs and their decisions. Often their board of directors, executive committee, and advisory counsel comprise almost, if not entirely, an inner circle stacked with those who cannot say no to their leader. The particulars of the institutions that operate this way make little difference; the one thing they all have in common is a not-so-happy ending.

The staff meeting under the tamarisk tree takes place in the initial days of Saul's full-out pursuit of David. This is when Saul is learning that David is not an easy man to corner. He also suspects that his entourage is not telling him everything they know about David, and that David must be receiving intelligence from some unknown allies on Saul's staff who are abetting his escapes by leaking military secrets. Saul already knew that Jonathan's allegiances lay with David, and he knew that it was Jonathan who had made it possible for David to make a successful escape before. This is why Jonathan is notably absent from this meeting, and why it's likely that he was no longer a regular member of his father's inner circle. Saul was obsessed with rooting out anyone else on his staff with divided loyalties like his son, so he cooked up a plan to purge any other collaborators before they set out on another search-and-destroy mission.

Saul had just gotten word that David and his men were now hiding at the cave of Adullam. While holed up there, David was warned by the prophet Gad to flee, so he led his men into the forest of Hereth. It's at this point in the pursuit that Saul set up his field command headquarters on the high ground of Gibeah, under the shade of a tree. We don't have any more details than the Scriptures provide, but if Saul was like other profoundly insecure leaders, I imagine the scene played out something like this...

Just before noon he sends one of his aides-de-camp to round up his senior staff for a meeting. They are told to report to the top of the ridge on the double, to the command headquarters under the cool shade of the big evergreen. Within the half-hour everyone is there, standing at attention in the midday sun waiting for the meeting to begin. But Saul is ignoring them. He is in the middle of a leisurely lunch over in the shade. He doesn't even look up to acknowledge or greet the men who have jogged up the hillside and are now standing about awaiting his orders.

We can almost smell the sweat pouring off his staff as the minutes pass. Their mouths have gone dry, they shuffle their feet, eyes down, silent except for the grumbling in their stomachs. Each man trying to figure out if he has forgotten some detail of his duty, or done something that might make him the next victim of the king's rage. They muffle their coughs and shift their weight from foot to foot, all while their leader fusses over some unseen detail of his meal. The only sounds are the buzzing of flies, the dull clink of gold and silver tableware, and the exaggerated smacking of lips from a man who enjoys eating almost as much as he enjoys tormenting his staff.

Finally he looks up, carefully daubing the corners of his mouth with a purple napkin. He tosses it down on an unfinished plate of food, flicks a couple of fingers, and the waitstaff hurriedly busses the table while he waits in silence. He glances over at his uncle Abner, the commander of his armies. But Abner stands like a statue, a warrior soldier awaiting his orders. "Good old Abner," he thinks to himself, and begins to speak.

The team braces themselves for what they know is coming. They clench their jaws and square themselves to absorb the tongue-lashing they are about to receive. Each man is silently praying that someone else will be the scapegoat this time, that someone else's family will be punished for his incompetence, that another man will be prodded and jabbed with the tip of the king's spear as he berates and humiliates him.

So when Saul begins to speak, they are surprised.

He's not yelling. He's sitting on the edge of his portable throne with his arms stretched wide, like a giant, kingly grandfather inviting a child to come sit on his lap. He holds his spear tilted harmlessly to the side. The unexpected change in persona has the entire staff reeling in confusion. It's as if their old friend and kinsman has suddenly returned to his senses and is once again speaking to them in civil and familiar terms. Note his fraternal way of addressing them as he begins.

"Hear now, O Benjamites!"

These opening words were carefully chosen to remind them that their entire tribe has risen to power and reclaimed their lost honor with his ascension to the throne. Undoubtedly, more than a few of his boyhood pals and relatives are there. Tribal loyalty was a powerful force in ancient Israel and still is in Near Eastern cultures to this day. Tribal loyalty is a kind of hyper-provincialism that regularly threatens national identity and supersedes any other allegiances; it's very possible, and even likely, that none of the other twelve tribes of Israel were represented in Saul's inner circle that day.

Next he asks a question they already know the answer to, gently reminding them that they are in a unique position to profit from their common ancestry.

"Will the son of Jesse also give to all of you fields and vineyards? Will he make you all commanders of thousands and commanders of hundreds?"

He nods knowingly at the faces in the meeting, his eyes inviting someone with real ambition to step forward, someone who knows how to take advantage of a once-in-a-lifetime opportunity when he sees one, someone, anyone, to step up and start talking. But no one says a word. They stand silently, too surprised and too afraid to say anything.

But the king's little game is far from over.

His voice rises, and the rage they were expecting jolts them back to attention. He accuses his entire staff of conspiracy.

"For all of you have conspired against me."

He stands up and points his spear threateningly around the circle, accusing them of abetting his rival, withholding intelligence, and sabotaging his military operations. He steps away from his throne and walks out to the nervous assembly. He looks down on the men he towers over, and settles his gaze on just one unfortunate soul. Staring at his random victim, his lips curl into a smirking smile. Almost instantly the man breaks under the king's powerful gaze; he looks away, choking back tears, and mumbles something about his proven devotion and unflagging loyalty.

Now the entire staff is reeling, bracing themselves for what they fear is coming, certain that the king has plans to punish all of them. A few eyes dart around the encampment, half expecting to see the king's private security force coming to pounce upon them at any moment. The king's voice rises again.

"And there is none of you..." The king pauses, moves back to his throne, sits down, and opens his arms again, and says in a voice barely above a whisper, "...none of you, who is sorry for me."

Suddenly his voice has a tear in it. The staff can barely believe their ears. Each man is doing his best to keep his face from cracking while his mind is racing. Each man is hearing a voice in his own head yelling, "You want us to feel sorry for you?" But these men know Saul all too well, so they keep their eyes forward, their backs straight, and their mouths shut. It's quiet again, except for the buzzing of flies. This is when an unfamiliar voice is heard.

"I saw the son of Jesse coming to Nob to Ahimelech the son of Ahitub."

A voice coming up from among the waitstaff and aides who are idling about the edges of the meeting. Saul motions for the man to come forward; he steps before the throne and continues.

"And he inquired of the Lord for him, gave him provisions, and gave him the sword of Goliath the Philistine."

Saul smiles broadly and turns to his staff with nodding and the upturned and pointing palm of approval that is the universal sign language for: "Now dis is what I'm talkin about!" He pinches the rat's cheek, gives him a love-tap slap, and says, "Heres da kind of loyalty I appreciate; a man who knows how to do some real denouncing and finger anyone who was collaborating with that son of a bitch son of Jesse."

But the rat was an outsider.

Doeg was from Edom. And because he was a foreigner, he was the only flunky under the tree that day who didn't already know that Saul couldn't be trusted. He probably couldn't fathom why no one in Saul's inner circle was jumping at the chance to claim some of the serious booty the king was promising for information leading to the arrest of David. So when no one else said anything, he jumped at the opportunity to speak up and gave the king exactly the kind of story he wanted, even if it wasn't exactly the whole truth.

When Doeg overheard their conversation and saw what happened that day, he knew that David had not told the whole truth to Ahimelech the priest about the exact nature of his business. But Doeg left out that important fact, knowing that to win the favor of a man like Saul, one needs to tell him only what he wants to hear. Doeg's intentional omission of the fact that David misled Ahimelech goes a long way toward explaining why he was willing to execute the priest of Nob when Saul's own soldiers were unwilling to do so. Even though Saul didn't believe Ahimelech's version of the story, Doeg had every reason to silence anyone who would have been able to refute his account later, including the innocent families of the priests.

But regardless of Doeg's motivation and his role in the massacre at Nob, Saul was the one who was convinced of the conspiracy. He had made up his mind, and the facts were not going to get in the way of his punishing those who had helped his enemy in any way. His inquiry ended in the cold-blooded massacre of eighty-five priests and their families. And while the men in Saul's inner circle were not willing to execute the innocent, there was not a single voice of dissent or a single thing any of them did to intervene. They were silent at the slaughter of all those men, women, and children.

This awful story gives us the opportunity to ask ourselves an important question. Have we surrounded ourselves with people who will confront us when we've done something wrong, or have we started to act like Saul and surrounded ourselves with people who will follow us blindly?

One of the wisest pieces of advice I have ever heard on this subject came from the Bible teacher Mike Webster. We were discussing how pastors and ministers who are transitioning from one church to another can know in advance whether or not the new pastor or leader they are going to be working for is a safe person, someone who will treat them fairly and with integrity. In the context of that discussion, Mike's crisp wisdom was, "Ask him who can say no to him."

This is a question we should ask ourselves. Who can say no to us? Who can stop our plans, change the course of our strategies, or hold us accountable for our actions? Or have we, like Saul, bullied and punished those around us so often that they've learned not to question or disagree with us?

Thoughts for Personal Reflection:

- Is it wrong to appoint family or friends to positions of leadership?
- What are some of the telltale signs of a leader who has stopped listening ?
- Give some example of family members who have successfully inherited their father's or mother's authority.
- Who are the people in your life who can say no to you?

Chapter 19

Blowing Your Own Horn

SECURE LEADERS DO NOT TAKE CREDIT FOR THINGS THEY DIDN'T DO

> *Jonathan smote the garrison of the Philistines that was in Geba, and the Philistines heard of it. Then Saul blew the trumpet throughout the land, saying, "Let the Hebrews hear." All Israel heard the news that Saul had smitten the garrison of the Philistines, and also that Israel had become odious to the Philistines.*
> *— 1 Samuel 13:3-4a*

The Story of Sumon

Sumon lived in the most beautiful village in all the land. A place where fat fish swam in the clear river that flowed from the snow-topped mountains. A place where melons and cucumbers grew all year long on succulent vines. A place that was never too hot, and never too cold. A place where doors were shut, but never locked. A perfect place, except for one thing.

Every few years people from the village would disappear and never be seen again. Sometimes a scrap of clothing or a fishing pole would be found. But mostly, when someone you knew went missing, he was gone forever. In those times, weeds grew thick in the gardens, fish went uncaught in the river, and mothers kept their children home from school.

This is what happened the summer of Sumon's sixteenth birthday. One day a village elder who went into the jungle to gather honey did not return home for his supper that evening. That night his old wife went from house to house asking if anyone had seen her man.

A few days later people from another village came, asking if they had seen a woman and her daughter who had left the week before to visit her sister. They soon discovered that the mother and daughter never made it to the village, and the missing woman's sister wailed so loudly that night that no one slept.

The very next day, hunters found tracks in the mud near a broken clay pot, tracks they said were from a tiger they were certain weighed more than five hundred pounds. It was then that mothers forbade their children to play outdoors, men were made to fetch the water, and the elders set about recruiting watchmen to guard the village at night.

So when the elders came to Sumon's home, his father presented his son, who had just come of age. Sumon and the other watchmen were to spend their nights in some of the large trees on the edge of the village. Each watchman carried a spear and hung a piece of iron from a branch that they were to ring loudly as an alarm to awaken the village if they saw the tiger.

Sumon was glad to be a watchman. He was proud to be old enough to climb into a giant old tree that was more dead than alive and to keep watch over his village through the long night. Up in the tree, all alone, he thought of the head elder's daughter and how she had smiled at him. He imagined waking up beside her in the same bed. These thoughts made him smile into the dark night.

But he also thought of the girl's father, the man who scolded him when he came near their home. He was asking a high price for his pretty daughter, and Sumon's mother said that the village women were gossiping about an older man who worked for the railroad and was bargaining with the father for the girl's hand in marriage as soon as she was of age.

The first few nights it was easy to stay awake. The fear of the tiger, the strange night sounds of the forest, and the thoughts of the girl kept him alert. Each morning when the sun came up, Sumon would climb down from the big tree and walk home with the other watchmen and talk with them about what they had heard and seen in the night. His mother would cook him some food, then he would try to sleep. Yet sleep was so hard with his little sister and brother confined to the house. But before dark, Sumon would return to his tree to sit in the moonlight and look for the tiger.

On the fifth night, Sumon was very tired. He had not really slept at all that day, and as he sat in the crook of that big dead tree, his eyes became like stones. When he could resist no longer, he drifted off to sleep while the full moon came up over the mountain. He dreamt of splashing in the river and of the girl's smile. He must have slept for a long time because when he awoke, the moon was high on the other side of the sky. He smacked his lips and shook the dreams from his mind. He stood up, stretched his arms, turned his head, closed his eyes, and yawned.

When he opened his eyes again, they became as big as the moon. Because standing on a limb, not more than ten feet away, was the tiger.

If the moon had not been so bright, he would never have seen the giant cat flicking its tail in the white light of the night. Its striped face seemed to melt into the deep shadows of the forest. Only the yellow of the giant's eyes allowed Sumon to know how very close the tiger really was. Sumon was frozen by its gaze; his mouth went dry, and his knees began to tremble.

Just then, like a clap of thunder when it is not raining, something passed by his ear, and he felt something soft brush against his face just as the tiger leapt toward Sumon. Then for a moment the tiger seemed stuck in the air, while feathers exploded and floated like snowflakes in the warm night. The limb broke with a crunch, and the tiger fell to the ground with a thud. Still more asleep than awake, Sumon somehow remembered to bang on the iron bar, but as he rang the alarm, he slipped and began to fall. As he fell, he reached for what he thought was a branch, but was in fact his spear.

He cartwheeled after the tiger and landed right on top of it. It flipped over in a final spasm of death, sending Sumon high into the air. Sumon, still clutching his spear, got to his feet and looked down at the cat, which lay motionless at his feet, except for the blood that was rhythmically spouting from a big hole in its side. He looked back at the spot where they had fallen and saw the limb with a broken and jagged branch sticking straight up. The branch was covered in blood.

Next to the bloody branch, a big owl also lay motionless on the ground. Sumon knew immediately what had happened. The owl had felt the tiger leap and had flown from the tree; the bird and the tiger collided in midair, and when the tiger fell back, the old branch snapped and impaled it right through the heart.

Sumon stood dazed and blinking into the slats of moonlight that were streaking the forest floor, trying to understand what had happened. Just then the men of the village came crashing though the brush with torches, spears, and the only rifle in the village.

They came upon Sumon standing with his spear in his hand, the tiger lying at his feet. The man with the gun fired twice into the tiger's side, then others came close with their torches to inspect the bloody hole in the heart of the tiger. They also saw that Sumon was bleeding; he had not felt it, but when the tiger flipped over, it unknowingly clawed Sumon across the neck and chest, leaving four long, shallow furrows across his body.

The men tied the tiger's paws together while another ran to the village to fetch a stout pole. It took four men to carry that tiger back into the village and two men to carry Sumon on their shoulders. The sun was rising as the men came into the village shouting, "Sumon has killed the tiger! Sumon has killed the tiger!" The villagers ran out of their homes as the women sent high-pitched trills into the morning light.

The tiger was staked out in the village center, and everyone came out to see it. Children hid behind their mothers, and just a few gathered their courage enough to run up and touch the soft orange fur of the fallen monster; then they ran back and cowered behind their mothers' saris as fast as they could.

The doctor came and bandaged Sumon's wounds, saying how fortunate he was that the tiger's claws had just missed the big vein in his neck. Exhausted, Sumon soon fell asleep, but when he awoke, the little house was surrounded by hundreds of people who had brought gifts for him and his family. They clambered about, asking to hear the story of how he had killed the tiger.

Leaning in the doorway, the white gauze in which the doctor had wrapped him streaked with four long red stripes, he stuttered and halted when he tried to talk. His tongue seemed much too big for his mouth; he wanted to tell the truth, but every eye was wide, and every ear hungry for a story. "Besides," he thought to himself, "What will become of all the wonderful gifts that my family has already received?"

Finally, he managed to tell a lie. How he had waited for the tiger to come so close that he was able to thrust his spear into the beast as it leapt for him. It was easy to lie; in the confusion of the night, no one had seen the bloody branch or the dead owl. It rained hard later that afternoon, so the next day when Sumon returned to the tree with men from the next village to tell the story again, all the blood was washed away.

After that, things went very, very well for Sumon.

The father of the girl came to the house to arrange a marriage to his daughter. The entire village built a house for him and his new bride. His father became an elder. The next year, his son was born. Soon he was telling the story to everyone who came to the village. Often, as he ended the story, he would take off his shirt and show off the four long scars that decorated his neck and chest like a bandolier.

Three pleasant years passed this way, until men from a village many miles away came to Sumon's house. They sat in a circle on the tiger rug that was on the floor of his front room. They called for the village elders and told of a tiger that was terrorizing their village. They came with gifts and money, begging for Sumon to come to their village and kill their tiger. Even before Sumon could answer, his father slapped his son on the back and said,"Of course my son will kill your tiger!"

The next morning Sumon kissed his wife and son, and the whole village shouted to him as he walked away.

Many years later, Sumon's own son was working with his grandfather to clear away part of his mother's old house. Under the floor, he found a small clay jar with a beeswax seal. He slipped it into his pocket, walked into the forest, and pulled out a piece of paper with the words "How the Tiger Really Died" written in large letters across the top. At the end of the story, he read his father's name and cried.

I think Saul was a lot like Sumon. A story got started that he was the one who defeated the Philistine garrison at Geba, and he never took the time and effort to set the record straight or properly laud the achievement of his own son. Then for the rest of Saul's life, the Philistines were the enemy he had the most trouble with, and the ones who eventually killed him.

It might also explain why the same army that so zealously followed him into battle at Jabesh-Gilead started to melt away from him on the eve of the battle with the Philistines, and why he felt compelled to offer the sacrifices, even though he knew it was so very wrong. This lack of confidence in dealing with the Philistines may have been the reason Saul's military leadership in this situation was suddenly so uninspiring; he unintentionally communicated his internal self-doubt to his followers. In critical situations, people seem to sense whether leaders actually know what they are doing or are merely BSing their followers.

Insecure people are thieves. They take things that don't belong to them. Insecurities can tempt us to take credit for things we didn't do. They can also tempt us to allow an inaccurate version of a story to circulate when it makes us look good or suits our personal agendas. It's amazing how quickly we'll act to correct an account of something that makes us look bad, and how slowly we move to set the facts straight when the account makes us look a little better than we really are.

Thoughts for Personal Reflection:

- How often do you laud the achievements of others?
- Is there someone who deserves recognition for an achievement that you avoided recognizing because they might be perceived as a threat to your authority?

Chapter 20

Isolation

Secure leaders have close relationships

The king sat on his seat as usual, the seat by the wall; then Jonathan rose up and Abner sat down by Saul's side, but David's place was empty.
— 1 Samuel 20:25

Samuel did not see Saul again until the day of his death...
— 1 Samuel 15:35a

Here is one of those delicious little details from the ancient narrative that gives us a glimpse of the paranoid king with his enforcer at his side and his back to the wall like a gangland mobster. He is isolated and lonely, but those feelings are not just something demonized and profoundly insecure monarchs deal with; they're an occupational hazard for all leaders. Most leaders find themselves living in the rarefied air of position, an altitude where the regular flow of friendships and meaningful relationships is not always easy to find. Yet find them we must. And just because combating isolation and loneliness is challenging for all leaders, it doesn't mean that we are doomed to spend our lives wheezing and gasping for life-giving oxygen, the friendships and relationships that we all need.

Profoundly insecure leaders remind me of the parable of the porcupines in Schopenhauer's *Studies in Pessimism*. The fable tells of an unusually cold winter when the normally solitary animals are forced to huddle together to stay warm. But in their communal attempt to keep from freezing, they quickly discover the pain of being so close to others who are just like them:

> A number of porcupines huddled together for warmth on a cold day in winter, but as they began to prick one another with their quills, they were obliged to disperse. The cold drove them together again, when just the same thing happened. At last, after many turns of huddling and dispersing, they discovered that they would be best off by

> remaining at a little distance from one another. In the same way, the human porcupines are driven together by the pressures of society, only to be mutually repelled by the many prickly and disagreeable qualities of their nature. The moderate distance that they at last discover to be the only tolerable condition of intercourse is the code of politeness and fine manners, and those who transgress it are roughly told — in the English phrase — to keep their distance. By this arrangement the mutual need of warmth is only very moderately satisfied, but then people do not get pricked. A man who has some heat in himself prefers to remain outside, where he will neither prick other people nor get pricked himself.[1]

Human porcupines. Wow, this is an image we would do well to keep ourselves from becoming. Prickly leaders with their own brand of barbed armor, forever lamenting their isolation, claiming to be misunderstood, yet all the while poking their subordinates and colleagues with their pointed words and deeds. Moving from one short-term friendship to the next, all the while gravitating toward organizations and systems that provide no meaningful accountability. Leaders like Saul, who have their backs against the wall and the quills of sharp spears at their sides.

Profound insecurity often manifests in isolation and is fueled by the fear of being fully known by those around us. Like Saul, all of us probably have some area of our lives that we believe must be kept secret. Insecure leaders are especially reluctant to associate with those who really know them, or as in the case of Saul and Samuel, someone they know to be prophetic. During the first two years of Saul's reign we find him in close proximity and association with Samuel. Notice that Saul's call-to-arms to rescue Jabesh-Gilead was a call to rally both himself and Samuel. The nation coming out as one man under the banner of both the king and the prophet is a beautiful picture of the cooperation and synergy of a multifaceted leadership team working in intimacy and harmony with one another.

The journey to isolation seems especially rapid for Saul. His failure to abdicate his throne to his rightful successor in a timely manner and his subsequent bouts with the demonic compelled him to distance himself from anyone who might know about the true condi-

[1] Schopenhauer, Arthur. Trans. T. Bailey Saunders. *Studies in Pessimism.* Swan Sonnenschein & Co., 1891.

tion of his soul. We have already seen how careful Saul was to keep David's real job at the palace under wraps, and how adroitly he probed Abner about how connected David's family was.

I suppose there has never been an easier time in history than today to have the appearance of meaningful friendships and true accountability while actually being completely unknown to those around us. Social media has made this so very simple – social intercourse without the risk of being known. We can take hundreds of pictures of our vacation, then spend days sorting and editing them and only posting the ones we want others to see. Gone are the days of awkward pictures of food being chewed with open mouths and un-sucked paunches. Today, we get to choose our most flattering pictures and to be seen with the people we want to be seen with. I'm not suggesting we post nasty pictures and go public with all of our uglier spiritual and emotional moments. But the question we must ask ourselves is whether there is anyone who gets to see us the way we are.

Remember that before Saul and Samuel parted company for the last time, Saul went up to Ramah, and the Spirit of God came upon him like He had on the day he was anointed. He prophesied just like he had in the beginning, but as we've already seen, the second encounter with the prophetic power of God looked very different because this was when Saul stripped off all his clothes before Samuel. We can only assume that his very public naked meltdown became a source of embarrassment for Saul and that he eventually lost all interest in being around the few men who knew what was really happening in his life.

By definition, isolated leaders are unlikely to have any legitimate check-and-balance personalities in their lives. They will usually surround themselves with conflict-avoidant friends or the kind of yes-men types we already talked about in the opening chapter of this section. Once this level of isolation sets in, leaders are already pretty far down the road to some kind of institutional explosion or personal implosion. Having people in our lives who really know us, can say no to us, and don't avoid tackling hard issues with us is the way we experience the kind of redemptive fellowship that is essential if we are to fully enter our destinies.

Towards the end of his life, David finally seems to have figured out that the friendship thing was actually a really big deal. It's interesting that in a lengthy passage that details all of the tribal leaders and David's cabinet members, including his treasurer, senior advisor, and general, is this reference: "and Hushai the Archite was the king's friend" (1 Chronicles 27:33). The NIV version of the Bible uses the word *confidant* instead of *friend* to translate the Hebrew word used here. The word carries with it the sense that this level of friendship was not just referring to a guy he played Texas hold 'em with once a month. Hushai was so much more – he was the kind of friend David could tell anything to, and also the kind of friend who would tell David what he really thought. I'm pretty sure if David had had Hushai around sooner, he could have avoided some of his own more embarrassing moments.

Thoughts for Personal Reflection:

- Do you have any life long-friendships with people who will talk to you about difficult things?
- Are there areas of your personal life that no one knows about?
- Are you keeping secrets from those with a legitimate right to know, like your spouse or spiritual authority?

Chapter 21

Monument to Self

Secure leaders do not build monuments and name institutions after themselves

Samuel rose early in the morning to meet Saul; and it was told Samuel, saying, "Saul came to Carmel, and behold, he set up a monument for himself, then turned and proceeded on down to Gilgal."
— 1 Samuel 15:12

The Peter School of Evangelism. Thomas Institute of Faith. Matthew's College of Financial Leadership. The Johannine Center for Love. It's impossible to think that any of the twelve men who walked the closest with Jesus would name an institution after themselves. To be fair, most institutions, buildings, new libraries, and the like are named posthumously as a classy way of esteeming and honoring beloved leaders.

But in this account we find Saul still very much alive. He's building his own monument to himself up on Mount Carmel, a high place of long-standing religious significance and eventually the site of Elijah's famous showdown with the prophets of Baal. It's curious that Saul would have chosen such a place to memorialize himself. There is no doubt that something had suddenly turned for the worse right around this time in Saul's life, because not too long before erecting this monument to himself, he had built an altar to the Lord (1 Samuel 14:35).

I would be very interested to know what that Saul monument looked like. Did he hire a sculptor to chisel his likeness out of marble or cast it in bronze? Or was it a simpler affair, like a commemorative plaque fixed on a big boulder? Or did he just hang off a cliff edge and spray-paint his name on the rocks? It would be so awesome if archaeologists were to dig up that monument, and who knows, maybe one day they will. There is also some very sad irony in the fact that his monument seems to have been lost forever. Because in the end, Saul was never forgotten; the problem is that he is most remembered for all the wrong reasons. His early victories and successes are all but swallowed up in the accounts of his failures.

Yet the yearning all humans have to be remembered is not a bad thing; it's actually a God-given desire for significance. It's why Moses prayed that God would give permanence to the work of his hands (Psalms 90:17), and why prehistoric people left their handprints on cave ceilings. We all understand the desire not to be forgotten. We all want to be remembered.

The first time I felt this God-given yen was when I was tearing down the lathe and plaster in an old house. This is when I found the names of two men written on a piece of plaster that had been hidden for almost one hundred years. They had used a thick pencil to say that they had done the wallpapering, then signed their names in the beautiful flowing script of the late nineteenth century. They must have written their names on the wall just before they brushed on the paste and hung the paper, because the plaster was like a perfectly sealed time capsule. When the paper and the plaster were separated by the pounding of my hammer almost a century later, it looked like it had been written the day before.

I don't remember their names, but I do remember feeling incredibly sad while I stood there and thought about them. I was sad because I didn't recognize their family names as being local; it was as if they had just evaporated off the surface of the earth. I was also sad because even though I was still a very young man, I realized maybe for the very first time that in spite of the fresh pink insulation and new drywall, someday someone would demolish my work, or maybe even tear the whole house down. After a little while, I used my own thick carpenter's pencil to write my name and the date on the back of that piece of plaster. Then I slid it back into the cavity of that wall, where it waits to be read by someone else someday.

So while I believe all of us can empathize with the desire to be remembered, or more precisely, the desire not to be forgotten, I honestly don't understand how someone could actually go through with building some kind of memorial to themselves like Saul did. Self-aggrandizement should wrinkle our noses like sour milk. And while having donor names etched in paving stones might not be exactly the same thing, I believe we would all do better to leave the business of our legacies to the crucible of history and the judgment of God.

Thoughts for Personal Reflection:

- Have you ever written your name in a place where someone would not find it?
- What is at the root of the nearly universal human desire to be remembered?

CHAPTER 22

Emotional Manipulation

SECURE LEADERS DO NOT USE THEIR EMOTIONS TO GET THEIR WAY

> *"For all of you have conspired against me so that there is no one who discloses to me when my son makes a covenant with the son of Jesse, and there is none of you who is sorry for me or discloses to me that my son has stirred up my servant against me to lie in ambush as it is this day."*
> *— 1 Samuel 22:8*

We began our look at the way insecure leaders hurt themselves under a tamarisk tree, imagining what Saul's staff meeting might have looked and sounded like. So it seems apropos to take our final peek at him under that same tree, during that same meeting, and focus our attention on how he used his emotions to manipulate those around him. When I hear Saul whining to his staff about how hurt his feelings are by their disloyalty, my imagination takes a darker turn; I see him wearing a diaper and sucking on a binky. In my mind's eye he looks like he had dressed up for a costume party, a giant man-baby with a hairy back and poopy diapers. I see him sticking out his bottom lip, throwing his teething ring while he cries,"None of you who is sowry fow me."

Sorry, Saul – save your tears for someone else. How could you, of all people, say such a ridiculous thing? It is beyond wacky for a despot like Saul to resort to using his emotions and feigning self-pity to get his way. He's about to order the senseless and heartless massacre of nearly one hundred innocent men, women, and children, and yet he's asking for, or at least pretending to ask for, the soothing comfort of having his staff feel sorry for him. Give me a break, you big jerk.

Saul seems to have been one of those folks who could turn their emotions, and even their tears, on or off with the flick of a switch. He could fly into a rage and spend months trying to hunt down David to murder him, and then break down weeping the instant he realized that David had in fact spared his life. Saul was little more than a method actor in a royal costume.

I don't think emotional manipulation is the most egregious manifestation of insecurity, but it might very well be the most terrifying. Not for the victims of manipulation, but for the leader himself, the person who has learned to access and enlist his emotions in an unwholesome and unholy theatric. Emotionally manipulative leaders like Saul don't start off in life with the intention of using their emotional outbursts to get their way, but at some point they learn that emotional displays can have a powerful effect on those they want to control. They discover that a red face and raised voice will cause people to back down in fear. They discover that a quivering voice and watery eyes will cause people to surrender their opinions and plans in order to assuage them with sympathy. They discover that emotions work like a charm, then learn to harness the powerful currents of emotions whenever they want to get their own way or get something accomplished. But manipulating one's emotions to manipulate others is a risky business.

The powerful emotional currents that are meant to authentically energize and animate our personalities and passions have the power to carry us off to a place it's difficult, if not impossible, to return from. Once we've lost contact with authentic emotion, once our feet are no longer grounded in sincerity and authenticity, we can be swept into a dangerous river where we don't know who we are or what we are really feeling.

Emotions are one of the evidences of the divine lineage of *Homo sapiens*, one of the things that make us human. Jesus, the perfect human, wept, laughed, and even got angry. Emotions are meant to be the involuntary responses to the births, deaths, weddings, defeats, and victories that punctuate our lives. Emotions are sacred. A beautiful facet of the human experience that reflects the Creator, whose image and likeness we bear, and who created us to experience the pain and pleasure of those emotions in their pure and untainted essence.

This is why the corruption of emotions – the dark art of being able to enlist them to assist us in achieving our personal agendas – is so very terrifying. Emotionally manipulative leaders can find themselves carried away like Saul, to a place where their own emotions have become just another weapon in their armory.

Thoughts for Personal Reflection:

- Have you ever used your emotions to intentionally get your way?
- If you have done so, how has that made you feel?
- Have you known someone who can turn on the tears?

Chapter 23

Hurting Their Followers

Secure leaders do not use intimidation or threats of any kind to get their way

As Samuel turned to go, Saul seized the edge of his robe, and it tore.
— 1 Samuel 15:27

But Samuel said, "How can I go? When Saul hears of it, he will kill me."
— 1 Samuel 16:2a

Not all insecure leaders have Saul's poor aim. They've thrown strikes with their spears and skewered their own Davids and Jonathans, pinning them to the walls of their homes, businesses, and churches. Yet in spite of his poor aim, Saul was able to do some real harm to those he was called to lead.

Bully This

"Don't you walk away from me when I'm talking to you."
"Don't you dare turn your back on me; we're not finished here."

It's easy to imagine Saul saying something like this to Samuel as the elderly prophet starts to walk away from him after delivering God's pink-slip prophecy to the disobedient king. When it came to the Word of the Lord, Samuel lived in a black and white, non-negotiable world. Since childhood, when word of God's disapproval of Eli came to him, he understood that after God spoke, the conversation was over. But not Saul; he had grown accustomed to having the last word and had been using his position and power to get his own way for many years. So when Samuel starts to walk away from him, he is not a happy king.

Saul is also a desperate man, and as we have already seen, he cannot and will not imagine his life apart from his position as king.

So the first thing he does is beg Samuel to forgive him and to return with him to worship before the elders of Israel for the sake of his reputation. But Samuel is not interested in any negotiation. He simply repeats the word of the Lord, and when he is finished, he starts to walk away.

This is when Saul gets physical. He grabs for Samuel, but catches the bottom of his robe in his big hands and yanks so hard that it rips. Now maybe Samuel's robe was a moth-eaten, threadbare antique he had picked up at the local thrift shop that was already falling apart when Saul grabbed it. But if it were in such a weakened condition when Saul grabbed hold, Samuel wouldn't have used the tearing of his robe as a metaphor for the violent rending of the kingdom that took place in the years to come. No, his robe was just fine.

Saul was just the kind of jumbo-sized strongman who could have pulled off this feat of strength. Maybe he used to entertain his staff by tearing the Jerusalem phone book in half or by bending steel in his bare hands. But all joking aside, consider how easy it would have been for a man of his size and stature to impose his will on those around him.

The same rage that boiled over against David and Jonathan erupts when he grabs after the old prophet. And apparently his bullying works, because Samuel eventually agrees and returns with Saul to put on a false face of unity for the elders of Israel. It's possible that he does it out of mercy or sentiment. But the Scriptures are clear about the fact that Samuel was intimidated by Saul, and soon after this encounter, he was afraid that Saul would kill him (1 Samuel 16:2).

We've already seen that in addition to being a physical bully, Saul was also an emotional bully. But notice that when he grabbed after Samuel, he caught hold of the bottom of his robe. He was either on his knees or on his belly begging for forgiveness when he grabbed the prophet. The disingenuousness of his piety was instantly revealed when he got physical the second he didn't get the response he wanted from Samuel. This is one of the amazing abilities real bullies have: the ability to flip a switch and change tactics instantly.

I don't believe Saul was always a bully; I doubt God would have chosen him to be king if he had been. But his disobedience changed him. Sin brings out the worst in all of us, and by the time he was fired from being king, he was already using his spear, physical strength, and emotions to intimidate and manipulate the people around him. Of course, not all bullies are bigger and stronger, or have the ability to go from sad to mad in the blink of an eye; they have different methods.

There are informational bullies who collect information, then glue together stories from the shards of gossip and broken pieces of conversations they love to overhear. Information and intrigue are their weapons of choice, which they use to blackmail those around them into doing what they want with subtle and not-too-subtle threats to tell others.

Some bullies use money instead of tears and spears. They attempt to steer institutions and people by providing resources for the things they want and threatening to withhold financing for the things they don't. This is why leaders with integrity don't allow themselves to be swayed by inappropriate pressure applied by those who hold the financial power in their institution. Leaders who pay too much attention to money run the risk of becoming the marionettes of those who pull the financial strings.

Some bullies even use their constituency to manipulate people. If you have ever been part of a church, or any institution, with stakeholders who are unhappy with the direction of the organization, these folks will often come to the leadership and say something like, "There are a lot of people who are going to leave or quit if you don't stop doing [or don't start doing]" whatever it is they are unhappy about. These are usually the words of a bully. They might not punch, scratch, or throw a spear, but make no mistake about it – they are trying to use the fear of a mass exodus or the fear of financial decline like a prod to move the leader in the direction they desire.

As a young pastor, words like "a lot of us feel that..." or "there are a bunch of us who want..." used to strike abject fear into my heart. Visions of empty chairs and unpaid electric bills would flood my mind. Next, I would try to connect the relational dots of the person who said that to me and try to figure out who the "a lot of" or "a bunch of us" actually were. I'm kind of embarrassed to admit it, but I used to lose a lot of and a bunch of sleep over those kinds of threats.

Then one day, when I was in one of those conversations and the fear started to rise up inside of me, I felt the Lord say, "Ask them who the others are who feel the same way." So I asked. Of course the bully didn't want to break a confidence and wasn't at liberty to give out the specific names. But he assured me in no uncertain terms that there were a lot of people who felt the same exact way. Later, when the dust settled, I discovered the "a lot" was only the wife of the man with whom I was speaking. This brand of bully will almost always attempt to inflate the size of his or her constituency to strike larger fear into the heart of the leader.

Thoughts for Personal Reflection:

- Has anyone other than a parent told you not to walk away from them after you have tried to end a conversation?
- Has anyone ever squeezed your hand too hard while shaking hands, or stood up to look down on you during a difficult conversation?
- Have you ever done either of these things?

CHAPTER 24

Disposable People

SECURE LEADERS VALUE THE LIVES AND WELL-BEING OF THOSE WHO DON'T FIT INTO THEIR PLANS

> *Saul said to him, "Whose son are you, young man?" And David answered, "I am the son of your servant Jesse the Bethlehemite."*
> *— 1 Samuel 17:58*

This may be the most perplexing passage in the Bible about the life of Saul.

Remember that David served Saul as his personal musician, then became his armor bearer, and the Bible says that "Saul loved him greatly; and he became his armor bearer" (1 Samuel 16:21). Later Saul sent a message to David's father Jesse, saying, "Let David now stand before me; for he has found favor in my sight" (1 Samuel 16:22). Then, just before his fight with Goliath, Saul actually attempts to dress David in his own armor.

The fact is, Saul knew David, knew his name, and knew who his father was!

So when Saul asks, "Whose son are you, young man?" the question sounds absolutely absurd. It sent me flipping back through the story to see if I had missed something. So I started studying and learned that skeptics and critics point to this passage as an internal contradiction and further evidence of the Bible's unreliability, and that Bible teachers and commentators have suggested several explanations for this seemingly inane and nonsensical question.

These explanations include: 1 Samuel is not necessarily in chronological order; David was coming of age and so now had facial hair that made him unrecognizable to Saul; and Saul's frail mental state was compromising his short-term memory. In my opinion, none of these explanations are very convincing or plausible.

So I would like to suggest a different explanation as to why Saul seems to have had a sudden case of amnesia about who David's dad is. In a word, Saul was already planning to throw David under the proverbial bus when he asked Abner, his trusted general, if he knew David's family. I believe Saul was simply trying to discover how connected David's family was and how David's demise or death would impact the delicate balance of tribal politics.

If Jesse's family had been well known to Abner, then Saul might have employed a different strategy for dealing with David. But by first discovering how well-connected Jesse's family was socially and politically to the upper echelons of society, Saul was able to more shrewdly plot out his next moves. If Abner had said something like, "Oh yes, I know that kid; he's the son of my old friend Jesse. I've spent many happy days fishing and hunting with him and his dad on their ranch, and I've known him since he was just a little whipper snapper. He's a fine young man, let me introduce you..." If Saul had heard something like that, we can be sure he would have proceeded differently.

But after David defeats Goliath, Abner innocently fetches David so Saul can find out for himself who the new hero's dad is. With David standing right in front of him, Saul has no choice but to pretend not to know him or his family, lest Abner suspect Saul was scheming something.

The fact that Abner didn't know David yet makes perfect sense, because we know that David's gig as musical exorcist was not something Saul would have wanted everyone to know about. This is yet another subtle genius of the Rembrandt painting – David playing the role of spiritual surrogate behind the curtain, in the shadows and out of the public eye. Not many senior leaders would be too keen on explaining to their staff that they have a demon issue.

One of the ways that profoundly insecure leaders injure those around them is to associate with them only when it advances their agendas or benefits them personally. Thankfully, most insecure leaders are not actually trying to plot the execution of their subordinates, but it still stings when we discover that someone we looked to for leadership is only interested in us as long we serve their purposes.

Thoughts for Personal Reflection:

- Have you ever felt like someone got rid of you the moment you stopped being an asset to them?
- Have you ever been thrown under the bus by a leader or boss?

CHAPTER 25

Name-Calling

SECURE LEADERS DO NOT USE PROFANITY AND STEREOTYPES

Then Saul's anger burned against Jonathan and he said to him, "You son of a perverse, rebellious woman! Do I not know that you are choosing the son of Jesse to your own shame and to the shame of your mother's nakedness?"
— 1 Samuel 20:30

Son of a ... perverse and rebellious woman. When we read Saul's words they might not sound like cussing, but they are. And we don't need a universal translator or a Hebrew lexicon to know what's going on when someone starts talking trash about someone's mother. These words were premeditated, vile, and intended to provoke Jonathan into attacking his father.

Saul broke the unwritten yet universal law that forbids speaking ill of anyone's mother, unless, of course, someone is trying to pick a fight, which is exactly what Saul was doing. This may be Jonathan's finest moment. Not many men could have shown such poise when someone was saying things like that about their mom. If he had taken the bait and come after his father across the table, Saul might have used sword or knife against him, but Jonathan stays in his chair and then walks away. This is when Saul, the rag-arm king, yet again missed the strike zone with his spear.

Cursing and verbal abuse is such a cheap ploy for trying to get one's way. And we're not talking about the kind of spontaneous cussing that might have erupted if Saul had just hit his thumb with a hammer and was doing a jig in the backyard. This was a dirty and deliberate attack on Jonathan that literally hit below the belt. Saul's cursing is full of sexual overtones, calling Ahinoam perverted and invoking the shame of her nakedness. It's why this passage ends with the note that Jonathan had been dishonored.

If anyone else other than his father had said those things about his mother, I think we can be pretty sure Jonathan would have come across that table so fast it would have made our heads spin. But

Jonathan was in an impossible situation; his demonized father was demonizing his mother, and he was in the middle of it all. If by chance you ever find yourself in a situation like this, do what Jonathan did. Just walk away. You can't talk reason with someone who is drunk, high, or just plain crazy.

Not only do insecure leaders love to curse and cuss, they also love stereotypes and labels. This is why Saul refers to David as the son of Jesse. Saul so loathed David at this point that he didn't want to hear his name spoken aloud. But for Jonathan and the rest of the nation, David is just David. He's the man who needs no last name. Like Elvis, Madonna, and Beyonce, David was the one-name star of ancient Israel before he became king, and his exploits were the stuff of legends. But Saul repeatedly calls him the son of Jesse.

By attaching David to his large family, Saul was attempting to cast him in the lead role of a larger conspiracy and insurgency. What Saul was trying to insinuate was that this son of a rival family with eight sons from the largest of all the twelve tribes wants to kick all of us out of power, take away all our jobs, and steal everything that we've worked so hard to achieve. If Saul had just called him David like everyone else, it would have meant acknowledging that this was really just about one man. It would have underscored what everyone else already knew – that the king had become obsessed with just one person, or as David would soon call himself, "a single flea" (1 Samuel 26:20).

This is why labels and stereotypes were, and are, an easy way to marginalize and discredit anyone who doesn't line up with our agendas or disagrees with our views. Labels like: those people, conservatives, illegals, liberals, gays, blacks, Hispanics, whites, Christians, Muslims. Classifications that strip individuality and heap humanity into big piles. And it's not just individual leaders who are fond of labels and stereotypes; institutions and movements love them, too. Organizations understand the deeply rooted insecurities of their constituencies and leverage those fears with labels and rhetoric that get votes, boost ratings, and increase giving. Labeling satisfies the appetite most of us have for simple solutions and easy-to-recognize good guys and bad guys.

It reminds me of the medieval view of the universe: the earth at the center, with the sun, five planets, and the rest of the universe revolving around us. It was an easy diorama to reconstruct, and it didn't rock the theological boat or established order of things. And if by chance anyone disagreed with the officially sanctioned model of the universe, the authorities just burned him or her at the stake.

Then this astronomer from Poland named Copernicus made some observations and crunched the numbers. Numbers that didn't happen to line up with the official model. Like all astronomers and astrophysics types, he was quite a clever guy, so he didn't publish his book until he was about to die. Thus he avoided being torched along with his book. But his mathematical proofs didn't die with him, and they eventually blew up the pseudoscience dogma that had been undergirding and justifying all manner of state-and-church sanctioned injustice.

Thoughts for Personal Reflection:

- Give some examples of modern stereotypes and slurs that we often hear.
- When are expletives most effective in getting people to do what we want?

Chapter 26

Relocations and Reassignments

Secure leaders do not relocate or assign impossible tasks to subordinates

Therefore Saul removed him from his presence and appointed him as his commander of a thousand; and he went out and came in before the people.
— 1 Samuel 18:13

Saul then said, "Thus you shall say to David, 'The king does not desire any dowry except a hundred foreskins of the Philistines" ... Now Saul planned to make David fall by the hand of the Philistines.
— 1 Samuel 18:25

I have a friend who had a falling-out with a new supervisor over a couple of answers she gave during a performance review. The answers weren't wrong, and certainly not the kind of thing that could get her fired; they just weren't quite the answers her new boss was looking for. The review took place on a Friday, and on Monday morning when she got to work, her boss greeted her at the door and informed her that her desk was being relocated.

Up until that day, my friend had been steadily climbing the corporate ladder and even had a coveted corner office similar to those of other executives with her responsibilities. But on Monday morning she was told to gather up her personal effects and move them to her new desk ... which just happened to be in a cubicle in the center of the building. She had been exiled to the middle of the office!

This relocation made my friend's job almost impossible. Detailed and important phone conversations were interrupted by the din of a busy office. She had to meet clients in a conference room that was not always available. But perhaps worst of all was the embarrassment of being relocated to a place that was designed to humiliate her and make her life miserable. So not too long afterward, when the company announced a downsizing and was offering some decent incentives, she jumped at the offer.

Relocations are often one of the first salvos fired by insecure leaders. David was reassigned to a lower-status position out of Saul's sight. My assumption is that his new posting was in a remote corner of the nation. You might know school teachers who lost the classroom they had taught in for years, or a sales team member who was reassigned a sprawling and lousy territory. Some employees have their parking spots changed. Maybe David came into work one morning and found his harps in a cardboard box and was escorted to the palace gates by security.

Insecure leaders fear being replaced, so they do all they can to avoid competing with subordinates. Not only will they relocate people they perceive to be threats, they often assign them to demeaning or impossible tasks designed to eliminate them or impede their progress. The subordinate's inevitable failure provides a ready excuse for dismissal, or at the very least puts black marks on their careers.

We don't need to sift through the Scriptures to discover what Saul was trying to accomplish by giving David the 100-foreskin assignment; the Scriptures tell us that Saul was thinking this impossible task would surely result in the death of David, because apparently men are not easily persuaded to give up their foreskins voluntarily.

My only personal vignette about an impossible assignment happened one summer when I was working as a carpenter's helper building houses. The carpenters I was working with were known as framers because they're the ones who build the frame of the house – the walls, trusses, rafters, and plywood sheathing. The boss wanted to get rid of me, not because he was particularly insecure, but because his younger brother was getting out of college the next week and needed a job.

So to have a good excuse for firing me, the boss gave me the impossible task of going an entire day without him being able to kick loose a single two-by-four that I had toe-nailed into place. For an experienced carpenter this was possible, but for an inexperienced helper like myself it wasn't. So it didn't take more than a half hour before he came along with his steel-tipped boot and kicked a two-by-four free from the plate I had improperly nailed it to. He let me work the rest of the day but told me I was through.

What I remember best about that day is not getting fired, but what happened at the end of the day. I didn't have a ride home, so the guys offered to give me a lift. But rather than driving right past my house like they had done before, they took a different route and dumped me about a mile away from home. The whole crew was snickering and guffawing as I jumped out of the back of the pickup and started my unemployed walk of shame back to the house with my tool belt over my shoulder. I'm just glad I didn't have to collect a hundred Philistine foreskins.

Thoughts for Personal Reflection:

- Do you have a story about being given an impossible job?
- Have you ever been relocated by a boss who wanted to make you quit?

CHAPTER 27

Verbal Snares

SECURE LEADERS DON'T ASK QUESTIONS IF THEY ALREADY KNOW THE ANSWERS

It came about the next day, the second day of the new moon, that David's place was empty; so Saul said to Jonathan his son, "Why has the son of Jesse not come to the meal, either yesterday or today?"
— 1 Samuel 20:27

Once a month Saul required his staff to attend several days of meetings, presumably to share intelligence and strategize about military operations and political policy. At this point in his career, David had already been reassigned by Saul to a lower-profile position that kept him away from headquarters. But in spite of his reassignment, he was still expected to attend the monthly staff meetings.

Surely Saul must have been suffering from some kind of severe mental delusion at this point, because the narrative makes it clear that he was actually expecting David to show up for the meeting. Remember, Saul has already tried to murder David three times by throwing his spear at him, trying to have him killed at the hands of the Philistines, and sending assassins to his house – and Saul was crazy enough to be earnestly expecting David to show up for the monthly meeting. We know this to be true because we have the benefit of knowing Saul's inner thoughts, and we know that he thought David must have had a legitimate reason for missing the first day.

Only after he is a no-show on the second day does it dawn on the delusional king that David is done making himself available for target practice and has finally fled from him once and for all. This is when he asks Jonathan why his buddy has not come over to the house for dinner. What was Saul expecting to hear his son to say? "Err...well... gee, Pops, I don't know why Davy is not at supper tonight. After all, Mom made tuna casserole, and that's his favorite."

But Saul asks his son the question anyway, even though he already knows the answer. Not because he wants to know why David isn't there, but because he wants to trap his son in a lie. And he does, because the two friends had already come up with a scheme that involved Jonathan telling his father a lame-excuse story about a Jesse family sacrifice that his buddy had to attend back at the family farm. I'm sort of surprised that the two of them didn't try to forge an excuse note from David's mom. But of course this is no game to Saul; he already knew that his son had formed an alliance with David, and he was just seconds away from attempting to murder his own son.

Profoundly insecure leaders are often conspiracy theorists, just like Saul. Their insecurities cause them to believe that everyone is against them, so they wage war against both real and imagined threats. Because they live in that shadowy realm, they are constantly probing for evidence of conspiracy and disloyalty in others. This is why they ask questions they already know the answers to.

Thoughts for Personal Reflection:

- When is it okay to ask questions you know the answers to?
- Is it healthy for parents to ask their children if they have cleaned up their room, or done some other chore, when they already know they have not?

Chapter 28

Harming Their Institutions

Secure leaders are able to take on new positions and new titles

> *"The Lord has rejected you from being king over Israel." As Samuel turned to go, Saul seized the edge of his robe, and it tore. So Samuel said to him, "The Lord has torn the Kingdom of Israel from you today, and has given it to your neighbor who is better than you."*
> *— 1 Samuel 15:26b-28*

After hurting themselves and their followers, it is inevitable that profoundly insecure leaders injure the institutions and organizations they have led. At best, the damages done are limited to the tenure of the insecure leader; at worst, they doom both the leader and the organization.

Inability to Accept Demotion

We've already looked at the topic of accepting demotion in our discussion of the insecure believer, but it's such a key element in the way insecure leaders function that we need to revisit the subject again from a slightly different angle.

When God asks someone to step aside or move into another role, it's not always because of some Saul-like sin. Most of the Christian leaders I hang around with are a lot more like Samuel than Saul. And while not a single one of them has a perfect track record, by the grace of God they've managed to steer through most, if not all of the chicanes and high-banked turns that have wrecked so many others. These are the leaders who have the greatest opportunity to leave a lasting legacy in their draft. The chance to accept new assignments, take on new roles, and continue their adventure down new highways and over new horizons is perhaps the most significant opportunity of all.

I'm certain that there are more than a few folks reading this right now who are in or near a season of transition. Transitions are opportunities, not indictments of failure. Opportunities to launch our successors into a higher orbit than we were ever able to achieve, and opportunities to model something that will make it easier for them to do the same thing when their time to step aside comes.

We've already seen how difficult it can be for the profoundly insecure to be disentangled from their titles and positions, and in those cases the inability to do so is an indicator of some pretty deeply rooted spiritual problems. So when we are in a season of transition, it's easy for all of us to misinterpret change as failure or rejection. But it's not; in fact, it is just the opposite.

Gracefully stepping away or aside from a familiar or long-held position of authority and power is something only secure people are capable of – people who understand that, at the core of their being, they are not the title they hold, nor are they the function they perform. They know that the same unknown, unproductive, and helpless soul who was loved by God back when their spiritual journey began is still loved by God the same way today.

I truly believe the story of Saul's life could have ended differently. I can imagine a scenario in which a penitent Saul humbly accepts the consequences of his behaviors, and his words of repentance just end with "Please pardon my sin." He could have voluntarily stepped down as king. He could have facilitated the peaceful transfer of power. He could have thrown his support behind the new and highly qualified king. He could have returned to some sort of semi-private life. He could have grown old and played with his grandkids. He could have.

This is a big deal to me personally. Immersing myself in Saul's story has forced me to look long and hard at my own insecurities and fears, and I think I've discovered that the things I fear most are obsolescence and irrelevance. I don't want to be like one of those broken-down pieces of farm equipment that gets dragged off into the brush line and eventually has trees growing through its gears. Nor do I want to become part of a movement that is something like a living history village where interpreters employ antiquated methods and antique implements to entertain tourists who take videos of how they imagine their great-great-grandfather did things.

As far as I can tell, the only way of avoiding the spiritual scrapyard or becoming an ecclesial vacation destination is by planning for succession long before it is forced upon us by death or decay. It's counterintuitive for sure, but by being both intentional and strategic in our planning, we have the opportunity to mentor and groom those who will take over our positions and carry on with our responsibilities. It also gives the institutions we lead the best chance of being more than a single-generation, one-off phenomenon.

With this in mind, here is a simple way to think about succession. Call it the three S's of succession:

- Strategy: A strategy is just a plan that takes a good deal of time and energy to develop. We don't need a strategy to decide where we're going to get lunch, but something like the timing and details of turning one's family business over to an heir or installing a next pastor is going to take more prayerful and thoughtful consideration. We shouldn't start thinking and making a wish about succession as we're blowing out the candles at our retirement party.

- Selection: Leaders who develop a strategy for succession have the privilege of being part of the process of selecting who will follow them. Moses took Joshua up the mountain with him, and Saint Paul took Timothy on mission trips with him. One of the primary responsibilities of leaders is the identification of future leaders. The prayerful, thoughtful, and careful selection of a successor is one of the greatest honors any leader can have.

- Support: Supporting one's successor involves many facets: education, training, and perhaps most important, the emotional, verbal, and practical support that will give our successors the best chance of success in their new roles. What leaders say is especially important, and how they respond to the critics of the new leaders may be the most important of all.

Successful succession is part of the great commission of Jesus to make disciples. Disciples are not dependents. Disciples are taught, trained, and then released to carry on the ministry of Jesus on the earth. One of the reasons Jesus made such successful disciples is that He stepped aside and sent them off in pairs to do ministry long before they, or probably anyone else, thought they were ready.

Thoughts for Personal Reflection:

- Do you have a strategy for succession yet? If not, when will you begin?
- How can institutions prepare for the inevitable change of leadership?

Chapter 29

Obsession with Dissenters

Secure leaders are not obsessed with those who oppose them, but stay focused on their institutional mission

So Saul arose and went down to the wilderness of Ziph, having with him three thousand chosen men of Israel, to search for David in the wilderness of Ziph.
— 1 Samuel 26:2

Saul was a man on a mission. The problem was, it was the wrong mission. So when he should have been fighting the nation's enemies, he was wasting manpower and resources on a personal vendetta. Like all insecure leaders, Saul was unable to tolerate dissent or differences of opinion. So when the surrounding nations were invading their territory, killing their citizens, and stealing their resources, Saul was off on a cross-country goose chase, trying to corner and kill the man with whom he had become obsessed. For years he doggedly pursued David, only temporarily pausing his pursuit when David twice spared his life and when the military incursions of the Philistines became too big to ignore.

Thankfully, not many leaders today outside of totalitarian regimes and crime cartels have the political power to hunt down and kill dissenters. But insecure leaders injure the institutions they lead when they become obsessed with those who oppose them, and misuse their energies and resources to root out and then ruin the reputations and careers of their opposition.

Because insecure leaders lack the ability to differentiate between a difference of opinion and a personal attack, they rarely consider opposing views or invite diverse opinions. This kind of monolithic mentality may very well be the behavior that makes insecure leaders the most dangerous to the institutions they lead. It's dangerous because so often the best ideas, innovations, and solutions get tossed in the dumpster along with the best people. The success of the institution takes a back seat to the survival of the Saul-like leader, who misappropriates all that time and energy obsessing about anyone who opposes him or offers different opinions.

It's a common practice for dissenters to be discredited as they increasingly become the targets of demotion or dismissal as their leaders become increasingly obsessed with their whereabouts and activities. Insecure leaders want to know who these people talk to at break and who they have lunch with. They become obsessed with the employees' time cards, where they park their cars, and even their personal lives.

Left unchecked, this kind of institutional totalitarianism will invariably lead to the kind of staff and inner circle of yes-men and sycophants that we observed in the first part of this section, and end with an obsessive attempt to destroy the reputation and life of the dissenter even after they're gone. Insecure politicians have used the power and influence of their offices to indict former rivals, and insecure pastors have written unsolicited letters to the new churches of former employees. It's an ugly business.

Thoughts for Personal Reflection:

- Have you ever become obsessed with someone?
- Have you ever been the target of someone's obsession?
- What role does bitterness and anger play in obsession?

CHAPTER 30

Stupid Rules

SECURE LEADERS DO NOT IMPOSE FOOLISH RULES AND REGULATIONS

Now the men of Israel were hard-pressed on that day, for Saul had put the people under oath, saying, "Cursed be the man who eats food before evening, and until I have avenged myself on my enemies." So none of the people tasted food. — Samuel 14:24

We've already learned that he United States Army estimates that a combat soldier needs up to 6,000 calories a day to remain in top fighting form. To give us an idea of how much food that is, it's the equivalent of eating ten Big Macs or thirty-nine pounds of broccoli. But regardless of how we slice it, combat is one of the most physically and emotionally exhausting experiences human beings can engage in, because it places demands on both the body and the psyche that require the maximum effort. Throughout history, military leaders have known that without proper rations, the health, vitality, and morale of their troops will quickly fade. When Napoleon famously quipped, "an army marches on its stomach," he was spot-on.

This is why Saul's command that his army fast during battle is so utterly, well, stupid. Israel was on the cusp of a complete rout of the Philistines, and Saul pulled the plug on the whole thing by having them engage in a religious ritual when they should have been eating. We've already seen how his insecurity-fueled obsession with success was so perverted that he was willing to sacrifice his own son for victory. But it's important to also note that religious leaders and communities are especially prone to creating and obeying similar kinds of rules for a couple of reasons.

First, it's easy to turn an unbiblical understanding of God into trivial pietism. This is what was happening to Saul throughout his life; he believed that sacrifice could replace obedience and thought that God could be appeased with religious observance. Religious practices are usually a pretty good reflection of an individual's or group's image of God. If we believe that God is a peevish deity, then we will probably embrace a peevish religious system in which the meticulous observance of religious rituals becomes extremely important. Whenever we start counting, measuring, or timing things like Bible reading, prayer, or hair length, we've probably made a pretty good start in engaging in a trivial expression of our faith.

If we're honest, most of us would probably agree that it's pretty easy to slip into a place where we're tempted to codify different aspects of our devotional life and worship habits. It's a bent in the human character that wants to convert our worship practices and lifestyles into a kind of predictable and permanent passcode that will open up the miraculous favor of God every time. Thankfully, He's not a keypad, and His favor can't be unlocked by punching in the right sequence of numbers.

Second, religious leaders and communities are prone to enact and obey trivial and foolish rules because well-meaning people in religious communities don't always have the courage to question a religious practice like fasting. Even those of us who emphasize the primary role of grace in the life of a believer probably find it hard to refuse a call to participate in almost any form of spiritual exercise. The real danger in this is when an insecure or bullying leader figures out they can leverage the call to religious activities to promote their own agendas. By turning the pursuit of God into a sort of piety contest where the person who stays on his knees the longest or keeps his belly the emptiest becomes the community's undisputed religious champion, who then gets to call the shots.

Religious rules and spiritual calisthenics can become a pretty effective way to intimidate and control the people around you, especially if they are part of an earnest religious community. Sometimes I've suspected that folks who appear to be very spiritual act that way not to please God, but to get their own way. They also have a tendency to tell everyone how much they've prayed about a decision, and if someone happens to disagree with them, they'll ask, "Did you pray about this?" in an oh-so-polite and yet clearly condescending way.

Ratcheting up the rules is also a way religious communities attempt to control and monitor their members. Institutions that are in decline and individual leaders who fear losing followers to other churches will often prey upon the sensitive consciences of their remaining members by instituting a series of ever-stricter rules and demands that are designed to keep the sheep from wandering into a different pasture.

I hope my suspicions are wrong, and we'll all have to wait until the furnace at the end of the age incinerates the combustibles in all our lives to discover even our own motivations. But until then, it would be healthy for us to understand that more rules and tighter regulations do not a healthy community or institution make.

The fewer the rules, policies, and regulations we enact, the better off we are. It's especially difficult to place very much serious weight on policy manuals and denominational credos that are actually longer than the entire New Testament. The lengthiness of these kinds of documents seems especially curious, if not downright spurious, when we read in Acts 15 that the apostolic leadership in Jerusalem settled the biggest crisis the early church ever faced with a seventy-two word edict - thirteen words fewer than this paragraph!

If we correctly understand and trust in the security that God is indeed a gracious Father, our religious practices will be way less inclined to focus on minute and trivial details. There is a unique sense of abiding security when we are led by the Spirit, which is so very different than the insecurity of being micromanaged by policy and dogma. Having a minimalist approach will also make it possible for secure leaders to attract and retain potential leaders with non-religious backgrounds, who are especially quick to recognize religious customs and practices that hinder the success of the institution.

Insecure leaders damage their institutional cultures by creating and implementing rules and practices that are designed to underscore and maintain the leader's absolute control, even at the expense of success and morale. Rules that are rooted in a particular culture, personal preference, or simply exist to extract thoughtless obedience will sabotage both the immediate success of the organization and its future success by driving off the next generation of potential leaders.

Thoughts for Personal Reflection:

- Can you give an example of something you consider to be trivial piety?
- What happens when rules replace character and leadership?
- How does the abundance of rules affect the recruitment and

retention of excellent leaders?

CHAPTER 31

Blame-Shifting

SECURE LEADERS TAKE RESPONSIBILITY FOR THEIR MISTAKES AND BAD OUTCOMES

> *The people rushed greedily upon the spoil, and took sheep and oxen and calves, and slew them on the ground; and the people ate them with the blood. Then they told Saul, saying, "Behold, the people are sinning against the Lord by eating with the blood." And he said, "You have acted treacherously; roll a great stone to me today."*
> *— 1 Samuel 14:32-33*

Old Testament dietary law forbids the eating of meat with blood in it. In order for meat to be fit for consumption, or what we call kosher, all the blood must be drained from the animal before it is butchered and prepared to eat. To properly slaughter an animal, a trained rabbi must slit the animal's entire throat with a single stroke of a square-bladed razor-sharp knife. The precise incision allows the beating heart to pump all the blood out of the animal quickly and humanely.

Please excuse the gruesome description, but it's necessary if we're to fully understand what happened the night Saul's starving troops started killing animals, and why this passage includes the detail about the men butchering animals on the ground. Simply put, livestock hastily slaughtered in the twilight by mobs of ravenous soldiers would definitely not have been in compliance with the dietary laws of the Old Testament.

When news of the non-kosher feeding frenzy makes its way back to headquarters, Saul immediately shifts the blame to the priests on his staff and then, predictably, accuses them of treachery. But as we already know, it was Saul's order forbidding his army to eat all day that was the real cause of this mass transgression by the famished soldiers, who were not about to wait around for the clergy to come and properly slaughter the animals. These men were way too hungry to care about the religiously correct way to bleed out the animals they were going to cook up for supper.

Later that same night, Saul makes a proposal that his armies continue to press their military advantage in a risky nighttime assault. This is when the chief priest calls a time-out and convenes a special service to inquire of God as to whether they should proceed. When there is no divine answer, Saul interprets this as evidence that someone has offended God by breaking the fast, and we've already learned that that someone turned out to be his own son.

I would suggest that the priest's sudden inspiration to hold a nighttime prayer meeting was not a response of earnest piety, but a response of fear. Remember, just a few hours before, these same priests had the blame for the illegal-butchering debacle shifted to them, so we can be certain that they were literally scared to death that they would be blamed if the night attack of the Philistines didn't go as planned. Even if God had spoken to them in the meeting that night, I'm not convinced the priests would have had the courage to report it to Saul. They wanted to have a prayer meeting not to inquire of God, but to avoid being punished or executed if that nighttime attack on the Philistines was just another miscalculation by their insecure leader.

It's also likely that this is why Saul put the idea for the night operation out there for discussion in the first place. If the raid on the Philistines was a success, then he'd be the hero. If the attack was a failure, then it would have been a simple matter to hang that failure around the necks of the same group of unspiritual priests who had already screwed up earlier that night.

Saul had created and cultivated a culture that made everyone around him more interested in covering their own arses than in focusing on the mission at hand. Tentative cultures and tentative people will rarely achieve significant things. Organizations with a culture of blame and blame-shifting become immobilized like Saul's army, and they are too sluggish to capitalize on the windows of opportunity that come along.

In organizations with cultures of blame, even small decisions are made to pass through a tortuous bureaucratic process – a process that documents every step and makes sure that someone other than the leader will be held accountable if something goes wrong. Children raised in blame-based family cultures become experts at tattling on their siblings to avoid being punished by parents who are more interested in fixing blame than cultivating integrity.

We have the opportunity to consider the cultures we are creating and cultivating in our families, churches, and institutions. Are we creating a Saul culture? One where the leader always seems to avoid responsibility for bad outcomes? One that is a minefield of trivial rules and regulations where people are so afraid of screwing up that they spend most of their time and energy trying to avoid failure and making sure they have someone to point the finger at if things don't go as planned?

Leaders of all sorts – moms and dads, pastors and elders, bosses and officers – all have the opportunity to create healthy cultures by lauding the achievements of others and accepting the responsibility for their own mistakes. Environments where people are free to focus on succeeding and achieving, rather than spending their time and energy avoiding being turned into human scapegoats upon whom the sins and mistakes of their leader are dumped, offer much more opportunity for people to achieve their goals and fulfill their missions.

Thoughts for Personal Reflection:

- Can you share an example of being properly credited for an achievement by a leader?
- Have you ever been blamed for something you did not do? How did you respond?

Epilogue

David's last encounter with Saul happens in the dark just before dawn. David and one of his lieutenants had snuck into Saul's encampment in the night and carried off a jug of water and Saul's spear from near the head of the sleeping king. Once he had safely climbed to the top of the other side of the valley, he yelled at the sleeping army to rouse them from their supernaturally deep slumber. Once they're awake, he mocks their general, Abner, for failing to protect his king in the night. He chides him for allowing him to walk right into their camp and steal the water and the king's precious spear that lay so close to his head. Upon hearing David's voice and realizing that he has yet again spared his life, Saul acknowledges David's righteousness and makes yet another empty promise to stop hunting him.

David then shouts across the valley, "Behold the spear of the king! Now let one of the young men come over and take it."

David knew that the spear was nothing he wanted any part of. It was Saul's personal property, and it wasn't the kind of trophy one takes home to put over the mantle. He knew that Saul's spear was more than a regular weapon, that it had become a totem for something much more deadly. So he lays it down on the rocks in front of him and waits for Saul's runner to come and fetch it.

David hears the courier long before he sees him. He tilts his ear into the shadows to make certain that the sounds of snapping branches and tumbling rocks is that of one man, and not a squad of assassins. By the time the boy scrambles all the way up the steep escarpment and breaks into the clearing where David is waiting, it's already starting to get light. Pink and purple clouds are stretching their spindly arms over the valley, and the songbirds are cheering on the sun in full throat. David had given the order for his men to move out while it was still dark, and so he's all alone as the boy makes his way toward him. The young man is drenched in sweat and breathing heavily when he stops a few feet from him with his arms akimbo. David can see the handsome young face awaiting his orders in the morning light, and he studies its earnest features for a moment, remembering his own thrill at being a young servant in the service of a king.

But he needs to go. His eyes point to the spear, which is lying on the flat rock between them. Surprised to see the weapon so close to his feet, the courier flinches as if he had nearly stepped on a snake. Then, after realizing what it is, he picks it up with both hands and looks to David for further orders. David holds the messenger's eyes in his gaze for a second, wishing he could invite him to defect and join his band of men. But the thought passes quickly, and David gives him the scram command with a flick of his eyes and head, and watches as the young athlete bounds down the hillside with the prize and disappears out of sight.

David waits only a few seconds longer, turns, and moves down the trail to catch up to his men. At first he's walking, but soon he is jogging, and as the sun breaks over the edge of the mountain, he is running fast, putting as many miles between himself and that damned spear as he can.

Acknowledgments

I want to thank Justin and Nicole Cober-Lake, whose friendship and editorial sensibilities made me look a lot sharper than I really am.

Thank you to Lorraine Roberts for taking the time to help me with typos and for asking lots of great questions.

Thank you to Bob Sorge, who saw value in this project long before I did.

Thank you to my daughters and their husbands, who bring great joy into our home and life.

Thank you to Neen, whose loving eyes have done more to heal my insecurities than any other earthly thing.

Made in the USA
Columbia, SC
30 March 2019